Two-Book Course in English, Book 1

TWO-BOOK COURSE IN ENGLISH

BOOK ONE

LESSONS IN THE USE OF ENGLISH

BY

MARY F. HYDE

AUTHOR OF " PRACTICAL LESSONS IN THE USE OF ENGLISH "
" A PRACTICAL ENGLISH GRAMMAR "
" WORD ANALYSIS," ETC.

ENLARGED EDITION

BOSTON, U.S.A.

D. C. HEATH & CO., PUBLISHERS

1910

646475

PREFACE

THIS book provides for three years' work, and is intended for pupils who are beginning to write English.

The leading aims of the work are to develop the child's power of thought, to aid him in forming habits of correct expression, and to give him a taste for good literature.

In the selection and arrangement of material, constant reference has been had to the needs and the interests of children. Such facts about the English language as are most essential to its correct use are given, and these facts are so presented that the pupil is led to exercise his powers of observation at every step.

From beginning to end, every exercise has a definite purpose and forms a part of a systematic and progressive plan of work. Some of the exercises are planned specially to secure accuracy of expression, others to give readiness and fluency of speech, and still others to increase the pupil's vocabulary and develop his imagination.

Provision is made for both a direct and an indirect application of the facts learned. The pupil is required to apply the different facts as they are presented, but his practice is not confined to the special exercises in which the various points are first considered. By means of simple exercises in dictation, reproduction, narration, and description, he is given varied practice in using the same fact again and again, that his use of correct forms may

iii

become fixed, and that he may be led to apply these forms unconsciously both in speech and in writing.

Throughout the book oral and written work are carried on together, the oral exercise being preparatory to the written one. In addition to this general oral work, special exercises in oral composition are given for the purpose of training the pupil in the expression of connected thought. These exercises, based on old fables and classic myths, will not only give the pupil self-possession and aid him in telling readily and accurately what he has seen, heard, or read, but they will also increase his vocabulary, train him in logical thought, and familiarize him with a large number of the best-known fables and myths.

The exercises in written composition are varied and lead to definite results. By means of directions, questions, outlines, or pictures, the pupil's interest is awakened, his thought stimulated, and his expression guided.

Special attention is given to letter-writing. Models of correct form are given, and the exercises are planned to secure ease and naturalness of expression.

Many choice selections from literature are introduced for the illustration or application of the principles studied, for memorizing, or for special study. These selections have been chosen for their special adaptation to the taste and the understanding of the pupil, and for their value in helping to form his taste for good literature.

SUGGESTIONS TO TEACHERS

IT is not expected that the exact amount of work laid out in each lesson will be all that is required for every class. Such additional exercises should be given as the needs of the class may demand.

All written work must be carefully done. Whenever the pupil constructs a sentence, whether to illustrate the use of a word or to state a fact, he should be required to do the work in such a manner as to increase his power of thought and to cultivate his power of expression. He should be inspired to put forth his best effort in every exercise.

There must be a constant application of the facts learned. The teacher should keep a record of the most common errors committed by the pupils in their written work, and should prepare simple dictation exercises containing the correct forms of the misused words or expressions.

When ready to give a dictation exercise, read each sentence slowly once (unless the sentence is long); then require the class to write it. In dictating a long sentence, a paragraph, a stanza of poetry, a letter, or any similar matter, first read the entire selection through, in order that the pupil may know what he is to write, and then dictate the separate parts in the same way that you would dictate a short sentence.

v

Much of the work, particularly in composition, is meant to be suggestive merely. All school studies afford good material for work in composition. Whatever the pupil is interested in, whether it be a topic connected with his reading, geography, history, nature, or other lesson, will furnish him a good subject for composition.

Pupils should tell and retell in their own words the fables and myths contained in the book, until they become so familiar with the stories that they can never forget them. There should be frequent repetition, also, of the poems that are committed to memory.

The sentences in large type are to be used in developing the various subjects. The pupils should read these sentences from the book, and should answer orally such questions on them as may be asked. The questions in smaller type are for the use of the teacher, but they should not be followed too closely. The teacher should add such questions of her own as may be needed to make the subject clear. After the pupil has been led, by means of questions, to see the truth presented, he should, without assistance, write the exercise which follows.

Attention to the language used by pupils should not be confined to the recitation period in English. Every statement made, every question answered in the course of a lesson in arithmetic, geography, history, or other study, should be expressed in clear, accurate, straightforward English.

CONTENTS

PART FIRST

PART THIRD

CONTENTS

PART FIRST

LESSON I

THE SENTENCE

Tell something about your book. Tell something about your pencil. Tell something about your desk.

Think of some object at your home. Tell something about the object. Think of something that you saw on your way to school. Tell what you saw.

Tell what you think about the weather to-day. Ask something that you would like to know about the weather to-morrow.

When you use words to express a thought, you make a **sentence**; as, —

1. The sun is shining.
2. The sky is blue.
3. Look at the clouds.
4. Do the clouds move?

Read the sentences. What is the first sentence about? What is the second sentence about? What does the third sentence do? What does the fourth sentence do?

A sentence is the expression of a complete thought in words.

EXERCISE

Copy these sentences.   Write your very best:—

1. Look at this butterfly.

2. It has bright yellow wings.

3. The wings are striped with black.

4. On what do butterflies live?

LESSON II

STATEMENTS

1. Autumn is here.
2. Crickets chirp.
3. The swallows have gone.

About what does the first sentence tell something? What is told about it?

About what does the second sentence tell something? What is told about them?

What does the third sentence tell?

Give a sentence telling something about your hat. Give a sentence telling what you like to do. Give a sentence that will tell your age. Give one that will tell where you live.

A sentence that tells or states something is a **statement**.

With what kind of letter does the first statement in this lesson begin? the second statement? the third statement?

What mark is placed after the first statement? after the second statement? after the third statement?

Every sentence should begin with a capital letter.

A period should be placed after every complete statement; thus,—

$$\textit{The wind blows the leaves.}$$

EXERCISE

(1) *Write a statement telling where the sun rises.*

(2) *Write a statement telling where the sun sets.*

(3) *Write a statement telling in what direction the sun appears to move.*

(4) *Write a statement telling one thing that the sun gives us.*

(5) *Write a statement telling another thing that the sun gives us.*

LESSON III

ORAL COMPOSITION

EXERCISE 1

Read this story:—

THE WIND AND THE SUN

The North Wind and the Sun had a dispute as to which of the two was the stronger. While they were talking, a traveller came in sight, and they agreed that the one should be called stronger who should first make the traveller take off his cloak.

The North Wind first tried his power, and blew with all his might; but the keener his blasts, the more closely the traveller wrapped his cloak around him. At last, giving up all hope of victory, he called upon the Sun to make a trial of his strength.

Then the Sun shone out with all his warmth. As soon as the traveller felt the intense heat of the Sun, he loosened his cloak, and soon flung it aside, hastening for protection to the nearest shade.

EXERCISE 2

Tell in your own words the story of "The Wind and the Sun."

LESSON IV

QUESTIONS

1. The horses ran away.
2. What made the horses run?
3. Did they run far?
4. Was any one hurt?

What is the first sentence about? What is said about the horses?

What is the second sentence about? Does the second sentence *tell* anything about the horses? What does it do?

What does the third sentence do? What does the fourth sentence do?

Ask something about a watch; about a kite; about a butterfly.

What is a sentence that asks something called?

With what kind of letter does the first question begin? the second question? the third question?

With what kind of letter should every sentence begin ?

What mark is placed after the first question? after the second question? after the third question?

The mark (?) is called an interrogation point.

An interrogation point should be placed at the end of a question; thus, —

Do you like to ride ?

EXERCISE

Write answers to the following questions. Make each answer a complete statement : —

(1) Where do we see the moon?

(2) How often do we have a new moon?

(3) Where have you seen the new moon at sunset?

(4) What is the shape of the new moon? Draw a picture of the new moon.

(5) Where have you seen the full moon at sunset? Draw a picture of the full moon.

(6) Where do you see the full moon later in the evening?

(7) In what direction does the moon appear to move?

LESSON V

SELECTION TO BE MEMORIZED

Read the following poem, and commit it to memory : —

LADY MOON

"Lady Moon, Lady Moon, where are you roving?"
"Over the sea."
"Lady Moon, Lady Moon, whom are you loving?"
"All that love me."

"Are you not tired with rolling, and never
       Resting to sleep?
Why look so pale and so sad, as forever
       Wishing to weep?"

"Ask me not this, little child, if you love me;
       You are too bold;
I must obey the dear Father above me,
       And do as I'm told."

"Lady Moon, Lady Moon, where are you roving?"
       "Over the sea."
"Lady Moon, Lady Moon, whom are you loving?"
       "All that love me."—LORD HOUGHTON.

The parts into which a poem is divided are called **stanzas.**
How many stanzas are in this poem?

LESSON VI

A PICTURE LESSON

How many children do you see in this picture? **What**
is each one doing?

Where are the children?   What do you see **around**
them?

What do you like best about this picture?

Write answers to the questions above.

SOAP BUBBLES

P. Wagner

LESSON VII

COMMANDS

Give a command that you might use in speaking to a dog; as, *Lie down.*

Give a command that you might use in speaking to a person; as, *Close the door.*

Give a request that you might make of one of your playmates; as, *Please hold my books.*

What request might you make of your teacher? of one of your parents?

Copy the commands and requests given above.   What mark is placed after each?

A period should be placed after a command or request.

EXERCISE 1

Tell which of the following sentences state something, which ask something, and which command or request that something be done: —

1. Look at the beautiful leaves.
2. Of what colors are the leaves?
3. Name a tree that has red leaves in autumn.
4. Name a tree that has yellow leaves in autumn.
5. Notice how rapidly the leaves fall.
6. What makes the leaves fall from the trees?
7. A few trees hold fast their leaves all winter.
8. What are such trees called?
9. Name two trees that are green throughout the year.
10. What are the leaves of the pine tree often called?
11. Draw a picture of a leaf.

Write a command or request that might be addressed to—

a soldier	a newsboy	a gardener
a sailor	a bootblack	a reader
a fisherman	a carpenter	a singer

(1) *Write a statement telling what your favorite tree is.*
(2) *Tell why you like that tree best.*

LESSON VIII

ORAL COMPOSITION

Read the following story: —

THE DOG AND HIS SHADOW

A dog, with a piece of meat in his mouth, was crossing a narrow bridge over a stream. Happening to look down into the water, he saw his own shadow, and thought it was another dog, with a piece of meat much larger than his own. He opened his mouth to attack the dog in the water, and so dropped what he had. He thus lost his own piece of meat, which dropped into the water, and the one he wanted, which was a shadow.

Tell in your own words the story of "The Dog and his Shadow."

LESSON IX

EXCLAMATIONS

1. Hark! what bird is that?
2. Hush! he will hear us.
3. How sweetly he sings!
4. What brilliant plumage he has!

What does *hark* express in the first sentence above? What does *hush* express? What word do you sometimes use to express the feeling of pain when something hurts you?

What does the third sentence do? How is the fourth sentence used?

A word or sentence that expresses sudden or strong feeling is called an **exclamation**. Exclamatory sentences usually begin with *how* or *what;* thus, —

How beautiful the moonlight is!
What a cold winter we have had!

What mark is placed after each exclamation above?

The mark (!) is called an **exclamation point.**

An exclamation should be followed by an exclamation point.

EXERCISE 1

Copy these sentences, and draw a line under each exclamation : —

1. Alas! what have I done?
2. Hurrah! our side has won.
3. There! I have spilled my ink.
4. Halloo! where are you going?
5. Halt! who goes there?
6. Ah! there he goes.

EXERCISE 2

Change the following sentences from statements to exclamations. Place the right mark after each:—

1. The children are happy.
2. The stars are bright.
3. I should like to go.
4. This knife is dull.
5. The boy rides well.
6. We had a hard frost.
7. This room is cold.
8. He must be a wonderful man.
9. The sun is warm.
10. This is a beautiful world.

Example. — How happy the children are !

LESSON X

THE PARAGRAPH

Notice how the sentences are arranged in the story on page 9 about "The Dog and his Shadow."

A series of sentences relating to a particular point is called a **paragraph.**

Tell how many paragraphs are in the story on pages 3 and 4 about "The Wind and the Sun," and what each paragraph is about.

A small blank space is left at the beginning of the first line in a paragraph. When a line is begun in this manner it is said to be **indented.**

EXERCISE

*Copy the story on page 3 about "The Wind and the Sun."
Do not forget to indent the first line of each paragraph.*[1]

LESSON XI

NAMES

What is your name? What is your father's name? Tell the name of some great man of whom you have heard.

What is the name of the place in which you live? Tell the name of some place that you have visited.

Name five things that you see in your schoolroom. Give the names of two kinds of flowers; of two kinds of trees; of two animals; of two parts of a house; of two pieces of furniture.

EXERCISE 1

Write in columns the names of—

(1) Five things that you eat.
(2) Five things that you wear.
(3) Five things that you play with.
(4) Five things that you saw on your way to school.

EXERCISE 2

Write the names of—

(1) Two trees used for shade.
(2) Two animals whose flesh is used for food.
(3) Two things made of iron.
(4) Two things that grow in the fields.

[1] To THE TEACHER. — Select other suitable paragraphs from this or other books for the children to copy, to impress the form and the idea of the paragraph.

EXERCISE 3

Write statements telling what the animals named below are covered with: —

horses   pigs   birds   porcupines

sheep   beavers   fishes   alligators

EXERCISE 4

Write answers to the following questions: —

What kind of food do cats get for themselves?[1] Why do cats need sharp claws? Of what use is the sheath which covers each claw? How is a cat able to walk without noise? Of what use are a cat's whiskers?

LESSON XII

HOW TO WRITE NAMES

1. Charles Adams is reading.
2. George Moore is making a kite.
3. Little Alice is looking at pictures.

Read the sentences above. Which words in these sentences are names?

What boy's name do you find in the first sentence? With what kind of letter does his first name begin? His last name?

What girl's name do you see in the sentences? With what kind of letter does that name begin?

Each word in the name of a person should begin with a capital letter.

[1] To THE TEACHER. — Let pupils answer these questions from observation. The answers should be written as one paragraph.

EXERCISE

Copy the following names of American poets:—

Henry Wadsworth Longfellow.
John Greenleaf Whittier.
James Russell Lowell.
Oliver Wendell Holmes.
William Cullen Bryant.

LESSON XIII

A PICTURE LESSON

EXERCISE 1

What are these children looking at? Where are the rabbits? Who carries the basket and why has she come here? Where do you think this little girl got her rabbits, and why does she wish to sell them? How many children are looking at the rabbits? Where do you think they live?

EXERCISE 2

Write a story about this picture:—

1. Tell who the little girl with the basket is and why she went out to sell rabbits.

2. Tell where she went to sell her rabbits and what success she had.

Meyer von Bremen

WHO'LL BUY A RABBIT?

LESSON XIV

GIVEN NAMES AND SURNAMES

1. That boy is Charles Taylor.
2. His brother's name is Henry Arthur Taylor.
3. He has a sister named Edith Taylor.
4. John Henry Taylor is their father.

What is the name of the boy spoken of in the first statement? Whose name is given in the second statement? What girl is mentioned in the third statement? Who is spoken of in the last statement? How does it happen that all the persons mentioned in the sentences have the same last name?

The name that belongs to all members of the same family is called the **family name** or **surname.**

The part of a name given to a child by its parents, or others, is called the **given name** or **Christian name.** The given name is sometimes made up of two words.

EXERCISE

Write answers to the following questions. Make each answer a complete statement: —

(1) What is your father's surname?

(2) What was your mother's surname before she was married?

(3) What are the surnames of five families that live near you?

(4) What is your father's given name?

(5) What is your mother's given name?

(6) What is your full name?

LESSON XV

HOW TO WRITE INITIALS

1. My father's name is James Richard Wilson.
2. He writes his name James R. Wilson.
3. My uncle's name is Charles Henry Ford.
4. He writes his name C. H. Ford.

What does the first sentence tell? What does the second sentence tell? What does *R.* stand for? What kind of letter is used? What mark is placed after the letter?

Whose name is given in the third sentence? Read the name.

What does the fourth sentence tell? What does *C.* stand for? What mark is placed after the letter *C*? What does *H.* stand for? What mark is placed after the letter *H*?

The first letter of a word is called its 'initial letter. What is the initial letter of the name *Richard?* of the name *Charles?* of the name *Henry?*

When, instead of a word in a name, you write the initial of that word, use a capital letter.

Place a period after each initial.

FXERCISE 1

Copy these names, and instead of the words in italics, write the initials of those words : —

Example. — Edith *Hart* Carter.
Edith H. Carter.

Edith *Hart* Carter.   Frank *Richard* King.
Mary Elizabeth Watkins.   Charles *Frank* Sherwood.
Alice *Carr* Williams.   Ernest *Page* Dalton.
Ellen Gertrude Lyon.   *John* Howard Miller.
Fanny *Lee* Robinson.   *Arnold Brooks* Sanford.

EXERCISE 2

(1) *Write the full names of ten persons whom you know.*
(2) *Write each of those names as the owner writes it.*

LESSON XVI

SELECTION TO BE MEMORIZED

Read the following lines, and commit them to memory: —

WHAT THE BIRDS SAY

Do you ask what the birds say? The Sparrow, the Dove,
The Linnet, and Thrush say, "I love and I love!"
In the winter they're silent — the wind is so strong;
What it says, I don't know, but it sings a loud song.
But green leaves, and blossoms, and sunny warm weather,
And singing, and loving — all come back together.
"I love, and I love," almost all the birds say
From sunrise to star-rise, so gladsome are they!
But the Lark is so brimful of gladness and love,
The green fields below him, the blue sky above,
That he sings, and he sings; and for ever sings he —
"I love my Love, and my Love loves me!"

—SAMUEL TAYLOR COLERIDGE.

LESSON XVII

THE WORD *I*

1. My name is James Gray.
2. I live in the city.
3. Edwin and I are playmates.
4. Edwin is larger than I am.

What name do you see in the first sentence? With what kind of letter does the word *James* begin? What is the first letter of James's last name? What kind of letter is that?

When you speak of yourself, what word do you use instead of your own name?

Who is supposed to speak in the first sentence?

What word is used instead of James's name in the second sentence? ·in the third sentence? in the fourth sentence? With what kind of letter is *I* written in those sentences?

The word *I* should be written with a capital letter.

Copy the following sentences: —

My name is Laura Bell.
I am eight years old.
I live in the country.
Miss Cary is my teacher.

LESSON XVIII

COMPOSITION

Write answers to the following questions. Make each answer a complete statement : —

1. What is your name?
2. How old are you?
3. Where do you live?
4. What is your father's name?
5. Who is your teacher?

LESSON XIX

NAMES OF CITIES AND STREETS

1. Harry Graham lives in Boston.
2. He lives in Beacon Street.
3. My cousin lives in New York.

What does the first statement tell? What is the name of the city in which Harry lives? With what kind of letter does the word *Boston* begin? Copy the word *Boston*.

What does the second statement tell? With what kind of letter does the word *Beacon* begin? With what kind of letter does the word *Street* begin? Copy the name of the street in which Harry lives.

What city is mentioned in the third statement? How many words are there in the name of that city? With what kind of letter does each word in the name begin? Write *New York*.

EXERCISE 1

Copy the following names of cities and streets :—

Washington.   Broadway
Philadelphia   Elm Street
San Francisco   Fifth Avenue
Chicago   State Street

EXERCISE 2

(1) *Write the name of the city or town in which you live.*

(2) *Write the names of the leading business streets in your place.*

(3) *Write the names of three streets in your city or town that are desirable for residence.*

(4) *Write the name of the largest city that you have visited.*

LESSON XX

COMPOSITION

Write answers to the following questions. Make each answer a complete statement :—

(1) What is the capital of the United States?

(2) What is the capital of the State in which you live?

(3) What is the largest city in your State?

(4) What is the largest city in the United States?

(5) What is the largest city in the world?

LESSON XXI

COMPOSITION

EXERCISE 1

Read this story: —

THE LION AND THE MOUSE

One day, as a lion lay sleeping, a mouse ran across his nose and woke him up. The lion laid his paw on the mouse, and was about to crush him. But the mouse begged so hard for his life that the lion let him go. Not long after, the lion was caught in a net laid by some hunters. He roared and struggled, but his struggles only fastened him more firmly in the net. Just then up came the little mouse. He went to work gnawing the ropes, and in a short time set the lion free.

What took place once when a lion was sleeping?[1] What did the lion do when he saw the mouse? Why did he let the mouse go? What happened to the lion afterward? How did the mouse repay the kindness of the lion?

EXERCISE 2

Write the story of " The Lion and the Mouse." First write the subject of the story, and then write the story in your own words.[2]

---

[1] To THE TEACHER. — The pupils should answer these questions orally, in complete sentences.

[2] Let the pupils read their stories to the class.

LESSON XXII

NAMES OF THE DAYS

Sunday
Monday   *Thursday*
Tuesday   *Friday*
Wednesday   *Saturday*

How many days are there in a week?

Name the days of the week.

With what kind of letter does the name of each day begin?

The names of the days of the week should begin with capital letters.

EXERCISE 1

Copy the names of the days of the week.

EXERCISE 2

Write in order from memory the names of the days.

EXERCISE 3

Write seven statements, telling in each one thing that you did on some day last week; as,—

1. Last Sunday I went to church.
2. I lost my knife on Monday.

LESSON XXIII

A PICTURE LESSON

THE FLOOD

EXERCISE 1

What do you see in this picture? Where are they? How did the dog's house come to be floating in the water?

What is the mother dog doing? How many puppies are there and what are they doing?

EXERCISE 2

Write a story about this dog and her puppies.

LESSON XXIV

NAMES OF THE MONTHS

January   July
February   August
March   September
April   October
May.   November
June   December

Mention in order the names of the months. With what kind of **letter** does the name of each month begin?

The names of the months should begin with capital letters.

EXERCISE 1

Copy the names of the months.

EXERCISE 2

Copy the following lines, and commit them to memory: —

Thirty days hath September,
April, June, and November;
All the rest have thirty-one,
Save February, which alone
Hath twenty-eight; and one day more
We add to it one year in four.

Notice on page 25 the little mark which joins the two parts of the words, *thirty-one* and *twenty-eight*. This mark (-) is called a **hyphen**, and the words formed by its use are called **compound words.**

The hyphen is used to join the parts of a compound word. It is also used at the end of a line to connect the syllables of a divided word. (See examples on this page.)

LESSON XXV

ABBREVIATIONS

NAMES OF THE MONTHS

The names of some of the months are sometimes shortened or abbreviated as follows : —

January, *Jan.*	July, *July.*
February, *Feb.*	August, *Aug.*
March, *Mar.*	September, *Sept.*
April, *Apr.*	October, *Oct.*
May, *May.*	November, *Nov.*
June, *June.*	December, *Dec.*

Observe that *May, June,* and *July* are not abbreviated in this list. The word *May* is never abbreviated; and *March, April, June,* and *July* are generally written in full.

The shortened form of a word is called an **abbreviation.**

What mark is placed after each of the foregoing abbreviations?

A period should be placed after an abbreviation.

EXERCISE

Write from memory the names of the months in order, and opposite each write its abbreviation, or, in those cases where that form is preferred, the full form of the word.

LESSON XXVI

SELECTION TO BE MEMORIZED

Read the following poem : —

THE MONTHS

January brings the snow,
Makes our feet and fingers glow.

February brings the rain,
Thaws the frozen lake again.

March brings breezes loud and shrill,
Stirs the dancing daffodil.

April brings the primrose sweet,
Scatters daisies at our feet.

May brings flocks of pretty lambs,
Skipping by their fleecy dams.

June brings tulips, lilies, roses,
Fills the children's hands with posies.

Hot July brings cooling showers,
Apricots and gillyflowers.

August brings the sheaves of corn,
Then the harvest home is borne.

Warm September brings the fruit,
Sportsmen then begin to shoot.

Fresh October brings the pheasant,
Then to gather nuts is pleasant.

Dull November brings the blast,
Then the leaves are whirling fast.

Chill December brings the sleet,
Blazing fire and Christmas treat.

—SARA COLERIDGE.

EXERCISE

Copy the poem about "The Months," and commit it to memory. Notice that each line begins with a capital letter.

LESSON XXVII

DICTATION EXERCISE[1]

1. January is the first month in the year.
2. February is the shortest month in the year.
3. March brings cold winds.
4. April showers bring May flowers.
5. June is the month of roses.
6. September is the harvest month.
7. October brings bright red and yellow leaves.
8. Christmas comes in December.

[1] TO THE TEACHER. — Read each sentence slowly *once*, then let the pupils write it.

LESSON XXVIII

THE SEASONS

What flowers blossom in spring?[1] What do you see on fruit trees? What do the birds do in spring? What does the farmer plant?

What kind of weather do we have in summer? What insects do you see flying about? What fruits ripen in the summer months?

What are the colors of the leaves in the early part of autumn? What becomes of the leaves later? What does the farmer harvest in autumn?

What kind of weather do we have in winter? What sometimes covers the ground? Why are the little streams said to be asleep? Name some of the winter sports.

The names of the seasons usually begin with small letters.

EXERCISE 1

Write answers to the following questions: —

What signs of spring have you noticed? Which birds came first, and when did they arrive? When did you see the first butterfly? What are some of the earliest wildflowers? Which blossom first? Which trees leave out first in spring?

EXERCISE 2

Write answers to the following questions: —

What are some of the common fruits of summer? Which ripen first? What are your favorite flowers that blossom in summer?

---

[1] Pupils should answer these questions orally, in complete statements.

EXERCISE 3

Write answers to the following questions: —

What birds leave your locality in autumn? What flowers blossom in the autumn months? What nuts ripen at this time? What wild animals are common?

EXERCISE 4

Write answers to the following questions: —

What have you noticed about the length of the days in winter? What holidays come in the winter months? Which season do you like best, and why do you like it best?

LESSON XXIX

ORAL COMPOSITION

EXERCISE 1

Read the following story: —

THE ANTS AND THE GRASSHOPPER

In a large field, filled with Grasshoppers, lived a family of Ants. The Ants were busy all day gathering grain for winter's use. When winter came, a Grasshopper, half-dead with hunger, begged the Ants for food.

"Why did you not store up food during the summer?" said the Ants.

The Grasshopper replied, "I have to spend my time in singing."

The Ants then said, "If you were foolish enough to sing all the summer, you must dance hungry to bed in the winter."

EXERCISE 2

Tell in your own words the story of "The Ants and the Grasshopper."

LESSON XXX

SELECTION TO BE MEMORIZED

EXERCISE 1

Read the following lines:—

SONG OF THE GRASS BLADES

"Peeping, peeping, here and there,
  In lawns and meadows everywhere,
  Coming up to find the spring,
  And hear the robin redbreast sing;
  Creeping under children's feet,
  Glancing at the violets sweet,
  Growing into tiny bowers,
  For the dainty meadow flowers:—
  We are small, but think a minute
  Of a world with no grass in it!"

At what time of the year does the grass come up?

What is meant by the grass blades' *peeping* here and there? Where have you seen the grass blades come up? Do you like to think of a world with no grass in it?

EXERCISE 2

Copy the "Song of the Grass Blades," and commit it to memory.

LESSON XXXI

COMPOSITION

A PICTURE LESSON

EXERCISE 1

Write answers to these questions : —

What does this picture represent? What is a man called that shoes horses? What is the room called where he works?

How do you like this horse? Why do you think he stands so quietly to be shod? What kind of disposition has he? What makes you think so?

What other animals do you see in this shop? What else do you see in it? What do all these things tell you about the blacksmith?

EXERCISE 2

Write a story about this horse.

1. Describe the horse, and tell what his name is.

2. Tell who his master is, what kind of home the horse has, and what he does.

3. Tell where he went one day, and what happened.

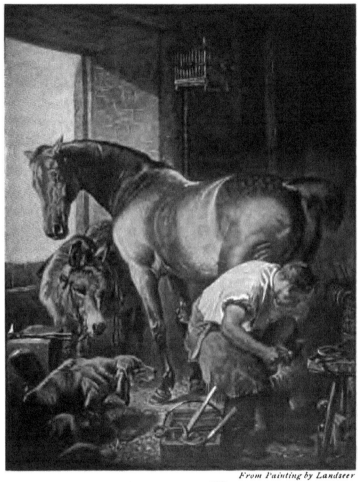

From Painting by Landseer

SHOEING THE HORSE

LESSON XXXII

TITLES

Mister, *Mr.*	Master
Mistress, *Mrs.* (mĭs'sis)	Miss

Which of the titles above are abbreviated? Which are written in full?

Mr. and *Mrs.* are titles used before names as a mark of respect or courtesy. *Mr.* is used before the name of a man, and *Mrs.* before the name of a married woman. These titles are written in the abbreviated forms *Mr.* and *Mrs.*

The title *Master* is used before the name of a boy, and the title *Miss* is prefixed to the name of any unmarried woman or girl. The titles *Master* and *Miss* are always written in full.

EXERCISE

Copy the following names. Do not forget to place a period after each abbreviation: —

Mrs. Elizabeth Barrett Browning
Mrs. Harriet Beecher Stowe
Mr. Charles Dudley Warner
Mr. John Burroughs
Miss Florence Dombey
Master Paul Dombey

LESSON XXXIII

THE WORDS *UNCLE* AND *AUNT*

1. Aunt Clara brought me a watch.
2. It was a present from Uncle William.

What is told in the first sentence? Who brought the watch? Copy the name *Aunt Clara*.

Read the second sentence. Who sent the watch? Copy the name *Uncle William*. With what kind of letter does the word *uncle* begin?

Give the name of one of your uncles. When you speak to your uncle, what do you call him? Write that name. Tell the name of one of your aunts. What do you call her? Write that name.

When you write the word *uncle* or the word *aunt* as part of a name, begin it with a capital letter.

EXERCISE

Write about a visit to one of your aunts. Begin as follows:—

My Visit to Aunt ——'s.

Fill the blank with the name of your aunt.

1. Tell where your aunt lives.
2. Tell when you visited her.
3. Tell what you did when you were there.

LESSON XXXIV

HOW TO WRITE DATES

1. Abraham Lincoln was the sixteenth president of the United States.

2. He was born February 12, 1809.

3. He died April 15, 1865.

Read the sentences. Who was Abraham Lincoln?
In what month was he born? On what day of the month? In what year?

In what year did he die? How do you know, from the third sentence, on what day of the month he died? How is the day of the month written? How is the year written? What mark separates the figures which tell the day of the month from those which give the year?

In the dates above, *12* and *15* are abbreviations of twelfth and fifteenth. These dates should be read not *February twelve* and *April fifteen*, but *February twelfth* and *April fifteenth*.

EXERCISE 1

Read the following dates correctly, and notice how they are written : —

October 12, 1492	April 30, 1789
December 21, 1620	June 17, 1800
February 22, 1732	September 3, 1808
April 19, 1775	January 1, 1900
July 4, 1776	December 25, 1905

EXERCISE 2

Copy the following sentences, filling the blanks : —

1. Columbus discovered America on October 12, 1492.
2. The Pilgrims landed at Plymouth on December 21, 1620.
3. George Washington was born February 22, 1732.
4. I was born —— ——, ——.
5. To-day is —— ——, ——.

Albany, New York,
October 14, 1909.

Dear Eva,—

I have two little kittens.
Their names are Buff and Gold.

Buff follows me wherever I go.
When I sit down, she climbs into
my lap and purrs softly.

Gold is afraid to come without
an invitation. She rubs against
my feet, and looks up into my
face longingly. Then I say, "Come,
Gold!" and she jumps into my
lap, and curls down by Buff.

Will you not come and see.
my kittens?

Your friend,
Emily Hall.

LESSON XXXV

A LETTER

Look carefully at the Letter on the preceding page, and notice its different parts. First comes the **heading**, which shows where the letter was written and when it was written; next is the **salutation**, consisting of the opening words; then follows the **body** of the letter, containing what is said; and lastly comes the **conclusion**, which is made up of the closing words and the signature of the writer.

EXERCISE

Copy the letter on page 37. Notice how the different parts are arranged, and place them in the same way on your sheet of paper.

Be careful to use capital letters and marks of punctuation as they are used in the letter given.

LESSON XXXVI

COMPOSITION

A LETTER

Write a letter to one of your playmates.

Tell about something that you have at home.

Begin and close your letter like the model given on the preceding page.

Use in your letter the name of the city or town in which you live, your own name, and the name of one of your friends.

LESSON XXXVII

ADDRESSES

The Address of a person is made up of his name and his residence; as—

1

Master Walter E. King,
60 Locust Street,
Toledo,
Ohio.

2

Miss Margaret L. Barton,
Haverstraw,
Rockland County,
New York.

When the words *street, avenue,* and *county* occur in addresses, they are sometimes abbreviated, as follows: —

Street	St.
Avenue	Av.
County	Co.

Sometimes the name of the State is abbreviated also. But it is better to write all these words in full.

Read the first address in this lesson. Whose address is it? What word is placed before Walter's name? In what street does Walter live? What is the number of his house? In what city does he live? In what State?

Read the second address. What word is placed before Margaret Barton's name? What does the second line of the address tell? What does the third line tell? What does the fourth line tell? What mark is placed after the first, the second, and the third line? What mark is placed after the last line?

If you were writing your mother's address on an envelope, what would you place before her name? If you were writing your father's address, what would you place before his name?

EXERCISE 1

(1) *Draw on paper two figures, each of the shape and size of an envelope. Make each figure about 5½ inches long, and 3¼ inches wide. Or, lay an envelope on the paper, and mark around it.*

(2) *Copy, in those figures, the two addresses given at the head of this lesson. In each, write the first line of the address near the middle of the figure, and be careful to place the other lines just as they are placed in the models*

given. Use commas and periods as they are used in the addresses given.

(3) Mark the place for the postage-stamp.

EXERCISE 2

(1) Write your own address as it should be written on an envelope. Write your real name, not your pet name.

(2) Write the address of your father or of your guardian.

(3) Write the addresses of five of your playmates.

LESSON XXXVIII

COMPOSITION [1]

Write letters from the hints given below. Begin and close each letter like the model given on page 37.

EXERCISE 1

JULIAN TO LOUIS

If to-morrow is a pleasant day, Willis and Julian are going to take their tent and camp out in the Maple Grove. They would like to have Louis go with them. Willis will carry their dinner in his father's old knapsack. Julian will take along his new book, "Hans Brinker," and he would like to have Louis take his bow and arrow with him.

Write the letter for Julian.

---

[1] To THE TEACHER. — Pupils should write letters as often as once a week, until they become so familiar with the proper form of a letter that they use it unconsciously. Always suggest to the pupil a subject that will interest him, so that he may write easily and naturally.

EXERCISE 2
LOUIS TO JULIAN

Louis would like nothing better than to camp out with Julian and Willis. He will go, and will take his bow and arrow with him.

Write the letter for Louis.

EXERCISE 8
RUTH TO BERTHA

It was so warm to-day that Ruth went to look at her pansy bed. She found the snow all gone, and the pansies in blossom. She sends some pansies to Bertha by Frank.

Write the letter for Ruth.

EXERCISE 4
. BERTHA TO RUTH

Bertha thanks Ruth for the pansies. She thinks they are beautiful, and she has put them into her little Japanese cup. She sends Ruth her last number of "St. Nicholas."

Write the letter for Bertha.

LESSON XXXIX

A PICTURE LESSON

Write answers to these questions : —

What do you see in this picture? What is the man doing? Why are the children so interested in his work? What other person do you see in the room? Why does she not watch the making of the cross-bow? What do you think the man will do with the cross-bow when it is finished?

F. Defregger

MAKING THE CROSS-BOW

LESSON XL

IS AND *ARE*

1. Herbert is in the house.
2. Herbert and Alfred are in the house.
3. The pencil is dull.
4. The pencils are dull.

Who is spoken of in the first statement? Who are spoken of in the second statement? Why do we use *is* in the first statement and *are* in the second statement?

What is the third statement about? How many pencils are spoken of? What is the fourth statement about? Which is used in stating something about one pencil, *is* or *are?* What word is used instead of *is* in speaking of more than one pencil?

Look again at the sentences given in this lesson, and tell when we use *is*. Tell when we use *are*.

Use *is* in speaking of one.

Use *are* in speaking of more than one.

EXERCISE

Copy the following sentences, and fill the blanks with is *or* are. *Be careful to use* is *in statements about one, and* are *in statements about more than one:* —

1. The bell —— ringing.
2. The sweet apples —— ripe.
3. —— your brother at home?
4. —— your sisters here?
5. The birds —— singing.

6. The eggs of the phœbe-bird —— snow-white.

7. The asters and the goldenrod —— in blossom.

8. The whale —— the largest animal in the world.

9. The elephant —— the largest animal that lives upon land.

10. The bison or buffalo —— the largest animal in America.

LESSON XLI

DICTATION EXERCISE

What is this little green tip peeping up out of the ground under the snowy covering? It is a young snowdrop plant. Can you tell me why it grows? Where does it find its food? What makes it spread out its leaves and add to its stalk day by day?

LESSON XLII

COMPOSITION

EXERCISE 1

Read this story: —

THE CROW AND THE PITCHER

A crow, perishing with thirst, saw a pitcher, and flew to it, hoping to find water there. He found a little water in the bottom of the pitcher, but it was so low that he could not reach it. Then he looked around to see what he could do, and spied some pebbles. He brought these, one by one, and dropped them into the pitcher, until the water was brought within his reach.

What did a crow see? Why did he fly to it? What was the reason that he could not get water there? What did he do?

Write in your own words the story of "The Crow and the Pitcher."

LESSON XLIII

WAS AND *WERE*

1. Agnes was in the garden.
2. Agnes and Alice were in the garden.
3. The bird was shy.
4. The birds were shy.

Who is spoken of in the first sentence? Who are spoken of in the second sentence? In which sentence is *was* used? What word is used instead of *was* in the second sentence? Why is *was* used in the first sentence and *were* in the second sentence?

What is the third sentence about? How many birds are spoken of? Tell whether we use *was* or *were* to state something about one bird. What is the fourth sentence about? What word is used instead of *was* in stating something about the birds?

In which of the sentences above is *was* used? How many things are spoken of in each of those sentences? What word do we use instead of *was* when we speak of more than one?

Use *was* in speaking of one.
Use *were* in speaking of more than one.

Copy the following sentences, and fill the blanks with is, are, was, or *were: —*

1. Carlo —— lonesome.
2. Fred and Harry —— away.
3. —— those marbles yours?
4. The ground —— covered with snow.
5. Horses —— first brought to America by Spanish explorers.
6. The llama lives on the Andes. It —— much larger than a sheep, and —— covered with long, soft hair of a brown or gray color. It —— used to carry burdens from place to place.

LESSON XLIV

REVIEW

EXERCISE 1

Use *is* in asking a question about an animal; about a flower.

Use *are* in making a statement about yourself and a playmate. Mention yourself last.

Use *was* in asking a question about a river; about the wind.

Use *were* in asking a question about the stars.

Use *were* in making a statement about two boys.

When should you use *was?* When should you use *were?*

What is a sentence that states something called? What is a sentence that asks something called? What mark should be placed after a statement? What mark should be placed after a question? What mark should be placed after a command? What mark should be placed after an exclamation?

With what kind of letter should you begin each word in your name? How should you write the word *I?*

EXERCISE 2

Copy the following sentences, and fill the blanks with **is,**
are, was, or were: —

1. The boy —— waiting for the basket.
2. The leaves —— falling.
3. A pigeon —— walking on the roof.
4. Two pigeons —— walking on the roof.
5. The larks —— ground-birds when they perch, and
sky-birds when they sing.
6. Have you ever lifted a stone that had ants under it,
and seen the ants hurry away, carrying little, roundish
white things to some safe place? People will tell you that
these little white things —— the ants' eggs. But they
—— not. They —— little white silk cocoons, and the
baby ants —— inside them.

LESSON XLV

ORAL COMPOSITION

EXERCISE 1

Read this story: —

THE BATTLE OF THE FROGS AND THE MICE

A mouse had been chased by a weasel and had just escaped,
very tired and thirsty. He was drinking from the edge of
a pond, when Puffcheek, the king of the frogs, asked the
stranger his name and the name of his father.

The mouse said that his name was Crumbstealer, and that
he was the son of Breadgnawer.

Then Puffcheek, the king of the frogs, invited the mouse, Crumbstealer, to his house, and offered to carry him there on his back.   So, Crumbstealer jumped on to Puffcheek's back, and they started merrily off across the water.   But when they had got out where the water was deep, what should they see but a great green snake.   It lifted up its head just in front of Puffcheek, and Puffcheek dived to the bottom, without stopping to think of Crumbstealer on his back.   And so poor Crumbstealer, who could not swim, was left to drown.

Now another mouse, Lickplatter, was sitting on the bank of the pond, and saw all that happened.   So he told the other mice, and they were all very angry.   They said that Puffcheek had taken Crumbstealer out into the middle of the pond and drowned him, and they declared war on the frogs.   They made breastplates out of the skin of a weasel, and they carried skewers for spears, and wore nutshells for helmets.

Then the frogs met together in council, and Puffcheek told the other frogs that he had had nothing to do with the death of Crumbstealer, but that Crumbstealer had drowned himself while he was trying to swim like a frog.   So the frogs went out to meet the mice in battle.   They carried radish leaves for shields, and rushes for spears, and wore snail-shells for helmets.

Then there was terrible fighting, and many mighty deeds were done on both sides.

At last, all the frogs would have been slain, if Jupiter had not interfered by sending an army of fearful monsters to their aid.   These creatures had eight feet and two heads; their mouths were like shears and their eyes were set in their breasts.   Men called them crabs.

When these frightful things came against the mice, pinching their tails and breaking their spears, the mice turned and fled, in terror.   And so the great battle ended, and the sun went down.

EXERCISE 2

Tell in your own words about "The Battle of the Frogs and the Mice."

LESSON XLVI

HAS AND *HAVE*

1. A squirrel has sharp teeth.
2. Squirrels have sharp teeth.
3. The boy has gone home.
4. The boys have gone home.

Read the first two sentences.   What is the first statement about? What is said about the squirrel?   What is the second statement about?   Which of these sentences states something about one thing? Which of them states something about more than one?   Why is *has* used in the first statement and *have* in the second?

Read the third and fourth sentences.   In which of these sentences is *has* used?   Why?   In which is *have* used?   Why?

Use *has* in speaking of one.

Use *have* in speaking of more than one.

EXERCISE 1

*Copy the following sentences, filling the blanks with **has**, **have**, **is** or **are**: —*

1. A true insect —— its body divided into three parts. Insects —— six legs. Most insects —— four wings.

2. Spiders —— eight legs, and no wings. The body of a spider —— divided into two parts. The spider —— not a true insect.

EXERCISE 2

Write answers to the following questions. Make each answer a complete statement:—

1. Into how many parts is the body of a fly divided? How many legs has a fly? How many wings has a fly? Is the fly a true insect?

2. Into how many parts is the body of a bee divided? How many legs has a bee? How many wings has a bee? Is the bee a true insect?

LESSON XLVII

COMPOSITION

Write something about your pets.[1] If you have pigeons, or a canary bird, or a dog, or a cat, or rabbits, write answers to the questions given on those subjects. But if you have none of the pets named in this lesson, write about the ones you have.

Write carefully, and be sure to begin every sentence with a capital letter.

[1] To THE TEACHER. — Before taking up this lesson, talk with the children about their pets. Find out what pets they have, and lead the pupils to tell about them. Then let each child write about his or her own pets.

The pupils should read their exercises to the class.

MY PIGEONS

How many pigeons have you? Where do they stay? What kind of house do they live in? Where is it? What do they eat? Are they tame? Will they eat out of your hands, and light on your shoulders? How do the old pigeons teach the young ones to fly? What do pigeons do when they are happy?

MY CANARY BIRD

Have you a canary bird? How old is it? Of what color is it? What is its name? Who takes care of it? What do you do for it? What does it eat? How often does it take a bath? How does the bird answer when you talk to it? Where do you keep its cage? In what part of the day does it sing most? How does it sit when it sleeps?

OUR DOG

What kind of dog have you? What is its name? Where does it sleep at night? How does it welcome you when you come home from school? How does it act when strangers come to the house? Has it any interesting tricks? What are they?

OUR CAT

What is your cat's name? Of what color is the cat? With what do you feed it? What food does it get for itself? How does it catch a mouse? What does it do with the mouse before it kills it? Where does your cat like to lie best? What does it do when it is happy? Tell any little story about your cat.

EXERCISE 5

MY RABBITS

How many rabbits have you? Where did you get them? How old are they? What do you call them? Where do you keep them? What do they like to eat? How did you tame them? Tell some interesting thing that they do.

LESSON XLVIII

WORDS TO USE WITH *YOU*

1. Has John a pencil?
2. Have the boys pencils?

About whom is the first question asked? If you should speak *to* John, and ask him the question, what would you say?

Read the second question. What would you say if you were asking the boys that question?

Did you use *has* or *have* with *you* when it meant one person? When it meant more than one?

1. Where is John going?
2. Where are the boys going?

Change these questions. Do not speak about the boys, but speak to them. Write the questions that you would ask.

Did you use *is* or *are* in your first question? Which of those words did you use in your second question?

1. Where was John last night?
2. Where were the boys last night?

What would you say in asking John the first question?   In asking the boys the second question?   Did you use *was* or *were* with *you* in your first question?   In your second question?

With the word *you* should we use *has* or *have?* *is* or *are?* *was* or *were?*

Use *have, are,* and *were* with the word *you* whether it means one or more than one.

EXERCISE

(1) *Write a statement, using you with* **have.**
(2) *Write a statement, using you with* **are.**
(3) *Write a statement, using you with* **were.**
(4) *Write a question, using you with* **have.**
(5) *Write a question, using you with* **are.**
(6) *Write a question, using you with* **were.**

LESSON XLIX

A PICTURE LESSON

Write a story suggested by this picture.

1. Tell who this little girl is, where she is, and what she is doing.

2. Tell what baby this is, and what the little girl does to make it happy.

Meyer von Bremen

THE LITTLE SISTER

LESSON L

QUOTATION MARKS

1. " Come and see the morning-glories," said Henry.
2. " Do they blossom every morning?" asked Ida.
3. " Yes," answered Henry.
4. " Let us count the blossoms," said Ida.

Whose words are repeated in the first sentence? Read the part of the sentence that tells what Henry said.

What question did Ida ask? Read her exact words.

When the exact words of a person are repeated by another, they are said to be **quoted.** The words repeated are called **direct quotations.**

What words are quoted in the second sentence? Notice the little marks that are placed before and after Ida's words. How are they made?

The little marks [" "] that enclose the exact words used by another are called **quotation marks.**

Read the third sentence. Why is *yes* enclosed by quotation marks?

Whose words are repeated in the fourth sentence? Read Ida's words. What are the marks called that enclose her words?

Every direct quotation should be enclosed by quotation marks.

NOTE. — In a later lesson, examples of quotations are given, in which the quotation is divided by other words.

EXERCISE

(1) *Copy the four sentences at the head of this lesson.*

(2) *Copy the following stanza, and learn to write it from memory : —*

The red rose says, "Be sweet,"
 And the lily bids, "Be pure;"
The hardy, brave chrysanthemum,
 "Be patient and endure;"
The violet whispers, "Give,
 Nor grudge nor count the cost;"
The woodbine, "Keep on blossoming
 In spite of chill and frost." — SUSAN COOLIDGE.

LESSON LI

THE COMMA WITH QUOTATIONS

1. George said to Robert, "Where is Bruno?"
2. Robert replied, "He is in the barn."

To whom did George speak? What did he say?

Read the second sentence. Whose words are repeated in this sentence? What shows that the words are quoted?

What mark is placed before the quotation in each sentence? With what kind of letter does the first word of each quoted sentence begin?

A short quotation, informally introduced, should be separated from the remainder of the sentence by a comma.

The first word of a direct quotation that is a complete sentence should begin with a capital letter.

EXERCISE 1

Copy the following story. Underline the quotations: —

THE FARMER AND THE STORK

A farmer set a net in his field, to catch the cranes which came to feed on his corn. He caught several cranes, and with them a stork.   The stork begged the farmer to let him go.   He said, "I am not·a wicked crane, but a poor, harmless stork."   The farmer replied, "That may be true. But I have caught you with the cranes, and you must die with them."

EXERCISE 2

Tell the story in your own words.

LESSON LII

DICTATION EXERCISE

THE FOX AND THE GRAPES

A hungry Fox saw some bunches of ripe grapes hanging from a vine high up from the ground.   He tried in different ways to get them, but wearied himself in vain, for he could not reach them.   At last he turned away muttering, "The grapes are sour and not ripe as I thought."

LESSON LIII

COMPOSITION

EXERCISE 1

Read this story: —

THE FOX AND THE CROW

A Crow stole a piece of cheese and flew with it to a tall tree.   A Fox, seeing her and wishing to get the cheese for himself, tried to obtain it by flattery.

"What a beautiful bird you are! what glossy feathers you have!" he exclaimed.   "If your voice were only equal to your beauty, you would surely be called the Queen of Birds!"

The Crow, highly pleased, opened her mouth to caw, when down dropped the cheese. The Fox quickly picked it up, and ran off.

EXERCISE 2

(1) *Tell the story in your own words.*

(2) *Write the story of "The Fox and the Crow." Be careful to use quotation marks if you give the exact words of the Fox and the Crow.*

LESSON LIV

THE COMMA IN ADDRESS

1. Horace, look at the falling leaves.
2. Come, Horace, let us gather the leaves.

Who is spoken to in the first sentence? What mark separates the word *Horace* from the rest of the sentence?

Where is the name of the person spoken to placed in the second sentence? How many commas are used to separate it from the rest of the sentence?

When you speak to a person, you are said to address him.

The name of a person addressed should be separated from the rest of the sentence by a comma or commas.

EXERCISE

Copy the following sentences, and insert the omitted commas and quotation marks:

Little Red Riding Hood met a Wolf, who said to her, Good morning Little Red Riding Hood.

Good morning Master Wolf said the little girl.

Where are you going? said the Wolf.

I am going to my grandmother's, said Little Red Riding Hood.

Where does your grandmother live? asked the Wolf.

On the other side of the wood, said the child.

LESSON LV

DICTATION EXERCISE

"Where are you going, my pretty maid?"

"I am going a-milking, sir," she said.

"May I go with you, my pretty maid?"

"You're kindly welcome, sir," she said.

"What is your father, my pretty maid?"

"My father's a farmer, sir," she said.

"What is your fortune, my pretty maid?"

"My face is my fortune, sir," she said.

"Then I won't marry you, my pretty maid?"

"Nobody asked you, sir," she said.

LESSON LVI

ORAL COMPOSITION

EXERCISE 1

Read the following story: —

THE HARE AND THE TORTOISE

One day a Hare made fun of the short legs and slow pace of a Tortoise. The Tortoise said, "If you will try a race with me I will beat you." The Hare, feeling sure that he could win, consented to try the race. They agreed that the Fox should mark out the course, and be the judge. On the day appointed for the race, they started together. The Tortoise never stopped for an instant, but went on with a slow, steady pace, straight to the end of the course. The Hare, knowing that he could reach the goal with but a few leaps, lay down by the side of the road and fell fast asleep. When the Hare awoke, he ran as fast as he could, but soon found that the Tortoise had reached the goal, and was quietly resting.

EXERCISE 2

Tell in your own words the story of "The Hare and the Tortoise."

LESSON LVII

CONTRACTIONS

1. I've torn the book.
2. Don't be careless.

What does *I've* mean in the first sentence?

Write *I have*. Write *I've*. What letters are in *I have* that are not in *I've?*

In writing *I've*, what do you place where the letters *h* and *a* are left out?

The mark ['] is called an **apostrophe**.

From what two words is *don't* made? Why is the apostrophe used?

Words, like *I've* and *don't*, made from two words by omitting a letter or letters, are called **contractions**.

An apostrophe should be used in a contraction wherever a letter or letters are left out.

Contractions are often used in familiar conversation, but they are seldom used in writing, except in poetry.

EXERCISE

Copy the following sentences, writing the contracted words in full: —

1. There's the postman.
2. Didn't you hear the bell?
3. Don't you like October weather?
4. Aren't the clouds beautiful?
5. I can't find the key.
6. It's on the shelf.
7. Isn't the room cold?
8. This coat doesn't fit.
9. They're coming to meet us.
10. Said the cunning Spider to the Fly:
    " Dear friend, what can I do
    To prove the warm affection
    I've always felt for you? "

LESSON LVIII

DICTATION EXERCISE

1. Doesn't the wind blow hard?
2. I'm glad that you're safe at home.
3. Couldn't you row the boat?
4. It's three miles to the river.
5. Here's a young robin.

6. 'Tis the early bird that catches the worm.

7. I've bought a pony.   Isn't he a nice one?   Wouldn't you like to ride him?

8. Where's the little boy that looks after the sheep?
He's under the haystack, fast asleep.

LESSON LIX

SELECTION TO BE MEMORIZED

EXERCISE 1

Read the following poem:—

THE BROWN THRUSH

I

There's a merry brown thrush sitting up in the tree;
"He's singing to me! he's singing to me!"
And what does he say, little girl, little boy?
"Oh, the world's running over with joy!
Don't you hear?   Don't you see?
Hush! look! in my tree.
I'm as happy as happy can be!"

II

And the brown thrush keeps singing, "A nest do you see,
And five eggs hid by me in the juniper-tree?
Don't meddle! don't touch! little girl, little boy,
Or the world will lose some of its joy:
Now I'm glad! now I'm free!
And I always shall be,
If you never bring sorrow to me."

III

So the merry brown thrush sings away in the tree,
To you and to me, to you and to me;
And he sings all the day, little girl, little boy,
"Oh, the world's running over with joy!
        But long it won't be,
        Don't you know? don't you see?
        Unless we are as good as can be."
                                    — LUCY LARCOM.

What is sitting in the tree? What is he doing? What **does the** thrush say in his song? Why was he so happy?

Where was the nest of the thrush? How many **eggs were in** it? What caution is given about the nest?

To whom does the thrush sing? What does he say to **every- body?**

Into how many stanzas is this poem divided? With what kind of letter does each line in this poem begin?

The first word of every line of poetry should begin with a capital letter.

EXERCISE 2

Copy the poem about "The Brown Thrush," and commit it to memory.

EXERCISE 3

Make a list of the contractions in this poem, and opposite each contraction write the words for which it stands.

LESSON LX

A PICTURE LESSON

Mme. Rouner

THE PLAYFUL KITTENS

How many kittens do you see in this picture? What are they doing? Where is the mother cat?

Write a story about these kittens.

LESSON LXI

ORAL COMPOSITION

EXERCISE 1

Read the following story: —

HOW APOLLO GOT HIS LYRE

The child, Mercury, was born in a cave among the mountains.

Before he was a day old he climbed out of his cradle and ran out into the sunshine. A pretty spotted tortoise-shell lay on the grass near the door of the cave. Mercury, seeing it, brought it inside. Taking hollow reed-canes, a piece of leather, and strings, he made a lyre of it.

Then he sang, and striking the lyre, made beautiful music all day long.

When it was beginning to grow dark, he stole out of doors again and went to the pastures where Apollo's white cattle were feeding. He chased them back and forth, and drove part of them away off into a cave and fastened them in ; but he had chased them in so many directions that their tracks looked as if, instead of going in, they had come out of the cave.

Then he went home, just as the light was coming in the east, slipped through the keyhole, climbed into his cradle again, and was soon fast asleep, with the lyre held fast in his arms.

Now Apollo was Mercury's brother. When he missed his white cows, some one told him that a baby had been seen, the night before, driving cattle, and Apollo went straight to the cave where Mercury lay in his cradle.

At first, Apollo was very angry. But Mercury, sitting in his cradle, his eyes sparkling with fun, played on his lyre and made wonderful music, sweeter than any that had ever been heard before. Apollo was so charmed by the music that he forgave his little brother.

Then Mercury told Apollo where his cows were, and gave him the lyre and showed him how to play on it; and Apollo, in return, made Mercury his shepherd, and gave him charge of all his flocks and herds so that he might drive them as much as he pleased.

Some day when the wind is blowing, and fleecy white clouds are flying before it over the sky, you may look up and see Mercury driving Apollo's white cattle.

EXERCISE 2

Tell in your own words "How Apollo got his Lyre."

LESSON LXII

REVIEW

EXERCISE 1

Write statements telling interesting facts about —

cork	pearls	coal	bananas
ivory	sponges	cotton	cocoanuts

EXERCISE 2

Use the following words in questions:—

is	was	has
are	were	have

EXERCISE 3

Write a command or a request about—

a horse	your hat	a fire
a door	your book	the tea-table

EXERCISE 4

(Dictation Exercise)

CAPITAL LETTERS

1. Broadway is the main business street of New York.

2. San Francisco has one of the finest harbors in the world.

3. William Penn founded the city of Philadelphia. The first streets were named from trees that grew on that spot. Some of these names were Chestnut, Walnut, Spruce, and Pine.

4. Benjamin Franklin discovered that lightning is a discharge of electricity.

5. Washington Irving wrote the story of Rip Van Winkle.

EXERCISE 5

(Dictation Exercise)

COMMA IN ADDRESS

1. Here, my friends, is a good place for our camp.

2. Mr. Bright, will you join our party?

3. Please, sir, can you tell me the meaning of this riddle?

4. Woodman, spare that tree!

5. Howard, what have you in that box?

6. Listen, my little hearers, to this story.

7. Blessings on thee, little man,
   Barefoot boy, with cheek of tan!

8. "Hush, Mabel, hush!" exclaimed the boy.

9. Ring, happy bells, across the snow.

10. Stay yet, my friends, a moment stay.

EXERCISE 6

(Dictation Exercise)

QUOTATION MARKS

THE BOYS AND THE FROGS

One day some boys were playing by a pond.

The frogs in the water lifted their heads and cried, "Croak! croak!"

"Oho! are you there? then we will stone you," said the boys.

So they began to stone the frogs, when a large frog cried out, "O stop! stop! this is fun for you, but it is death for us."

Then the boys saw how cruel they had been, and left the frogs in peace.

EXERCISE 7

LETTER-WRITING

Write a letter to one of your cousins, telling how you spent your summer vacation.

SUMMARY OF RULES

NOTE. — The pupil should apply these rules in all written exercises.

Every sentence should begin with a capital letter.

Each word in the name of a person should begin with a capital letter.

The word *I* should be written with a capital letter.

The name of a city or of a street should begin with a capital letter.

The names of the days of the week should begin with capital letters.

The names of the months should begin with capital letters.

The names of the seasons usually begin with small letters.

The first word of a direct quotation that is a complete sentence should begin with a capital letter.

The first word of every line of poetry should begin with a capital letter.

A period should be placed after every complete statement and after every command.

An interrogation point should be placed after a question.

An exclamation should be followed by an exclamation point.

A period should be placed after an abbreviation.

The name of a person addressed should be separated from the rest of the sentence by a comma or commas.

A short quotation informally introduced should be separated from the remainder of the sentence by a comma.

Every direct quotation should be enclosed by quotation marks.

An apostrophe should be used in a contraction, wherever a letter or letters are left out.

The hyphen is used to join the parts of a compound word.

The hyphen is used at the end of a line to connect the syllables of a divided word.

PART SECOND

---◦◦◦---

LESSON LXIII

THE TWO PARTS OF A STATEMENT

1. Plants need sunshine.
2. Two trains crossed the bridge.
3. The bell is ringing.

What are spoken of in the first statement? What is said about plants?

What are spoken of in the second statement? What is said about two trains?

What is spoken of in the third statement? What is said about the bell?

How many parts has each statement? What does one part show? What does the other part tell?

Name the two parts of each statement above.

Every statement is made up of two parts. One part names that about which something is said; the other part tells what is said about the thing named.

EXERCISE

Copy the following statements, and draw a short vertical line between the two parts of each statement:—

Example.—Oranges | grow in Florida.

1. Oranges grow in Florida.
2. The ground is covered with snow.
3. Walter is sweeping the walk.
4. Two little sparrows came to my window.
5. Emily gave the birds some crumbs.
6. This apple is hard.
7. Your pencil has a sharp point.
8. A small boy opened the gate.
9. The room has three windows.
10. The old clock stands in the hall.

LESSON LXIV

NAMES

1. John harnessed the horse.
2. Flour is made into bread.
3. The robin is building a nest.

Tell what is spoken of in each statement, and what is said about the thing spoken of.

Point out each word used as a name, and tell what it is the name of.

A word used as a name is a *noun*.

EXERCISE 1

Write sentences containing the following words used as nouns:—

table	river	lily	barn	grass
carpet	pond	potato	post-office	clouds

Write sentences containing the name of —

1. A flower.
2. A body of water.
3. An article of furniture.
4. A kind of grain.
5. A musical instrument.
6. A timepiece.
7. A vegetable used for food.
8. A building used for residence.
9. A building used for worship.
10. A material of which stoves are made.

Example. — The dandelion grows by the roadside.

LESSON LXV

PROPER AND COMMON NAMES

Give the name of a boy; of a city; of a river.

A name that belongs to an individual person or thing is called a **proper name**; as, *Frank, Charleston, Red River.*

Give a name applied to animals of the same kind — to a class of animals; as, *cow.*

Give a name applied to each bird of some class; to each tree of some class; to each building of some class.

A name that all things of the same class have in common is called a **common name**; as, *man, house, horse.*

Tell which of the following names are common to persons or things of the same class, and which belong to individual persons or things: —

house	school	boy	Germany
city	Yale College	Robert	month
Chicago	state	girl	January
church	Kentucky	Helen	day
Trinity Church	river	country	Tuesday

With what kind of letters do the examples of common names begin? With what kind of letters do the examples of proper names begin?

A proper name should begin with a capital letter; as, *James, Broadway.*

When a proper name is made up of two or more words, each word should generally begin with a capital letter; as, *New York, Niagara Falls.*

EXERCISE 1

Copy these sentences, and draw lines under the words that name special persons or things: —

1. Mount Vernon was the home of George Washington.
2. Edward is learning to play the flute.
3. Uncle Robert has gone to Europe.
4. Umbrellas were introduced into England from China.
5. We walked through Central Park.
6. Yellowstone Park contains some of the most wonderful geysers in the world.
7. Our friends are staying at the Holland House.
8. The concert was held in Steinway Hall.
9. Lake George is noted for its beautiful scenery.

EXERCISE 2

Write a few interesting facts about —

the city or town, the county, or the State, — in which you live.

LESSON LXVI

ORAL COMPOSITION

EXERCISE 1

Read the following story : —

PHAETHON[1]

Phaethon was the son of Helios,[2] the sun-god.

His companions would not believe that he was the son of the great Helios, who drives the shining chariot of the sun over the earth, and so Phaethon one day went to the golden palace of the sun and asked Helios for some proof that he was his father.

Helios, dressed in royal purple, was sitting on his throne, and he welcomed Phaethon, and told him, at once, that he was his father, and for proof, swore by the river Styx, that whatsoever Phaethon might ask of him should be granted.

Phaethon immediately asked, with great eagerness, that he might be allowed to drive the horses of the sun for one day.

Then Helios was sorry that he had taken such an oath. He told Phaethon the dangers of driving those spirited horses that breathe sparks of fire from their nostrils, and of

[1] Phaethon (fā'-ē-thŏn).　　　　[2] Helios (hē'-lǐ-ŏs).

the dangers of the road he must travel. But Phaethon only put his arms around his father's neck and begged the harder. So when Aurora drew back the purple curtains of the dawn, and the Hours harnessed the fire-breathing horses to the chariot of the sun, Helios — because he had sworn by the river Styx — allowed Phaethon to take the reins.

Phaethon jumped quickly into the chariot. But the horses, at once, missed the strong hand of their master, and plunged out of the road, snorting and rearing. The chariot of the sun flew, first, far away from the earth, and then close to it. It finally came so close, that rivers were dried up, the whole country called Libya became a desert, mountain tops took fire, and in some places the heat was so great that the people on the earth were scorched to a black color.

Jupiter, looking down from his throne, saw the world on fire, and he hurled a thunderbolt and struck Phaethon from the chariot.

Then Phaethon fell, straight down, like a falling star, into the river Eridanus. His sisters wept for him a long time on its banks, and they were finally turned into larch trees. As their tears fell into the water, Helios changed them into drops of amber, and larch trees weep tears of amber to this day.

EXERCISE 2

Point out the proper names in this story.

EXERCISE 3

Tell in your own words the story of "Phaethon."

LESSON LXVII

WHEN TO USE CAPITAL LETTERS

I

Tell which words in the following sentences are used as titles, and point out each title that is applied to an individual : —

1. The boy was welcomed by aunts, uncles, and cousins.

2. He stood by Uncle William.

3. The fathers and the mothers of the children were invited.

4. Here are your slippers, Father.

5. Senator Brown made a speech.

6. Two generals were on the train.

7. General Warren was killed at the battle of Bunker Hill.

8. The Governor of Vermont signed the bill.

9. The Pope lives at Rome.

10. The eldest son of King Edward is called the Prince of Wales.

When a title is applied to an individual, or when it is used as part of a name, it should begin with a capital letter ; as, —

The Mayor of Chicago   President Lincoln   Aunt Mildred

II

1. The Republicans held a meeting last evening.

2. Mr. Brown is a Baptist.

3. Congress meets the first Monday in December.

What is *Republicans* the name of? What is *Baptist* the name of? What is *Congress* the name of?

Begin with a capital letter the name of a religious sect, of a political party, or of any special body of men; as,—

> *Presbyterian*   *Democrat*   *Congress*

III

Find in these sentences the name of a document of special importance, the name of an important event, and the title of a book:—

1. This law is contrary to the Constitution of the United States.

2. Here was fought a great battle of the Revolution.

3. Have you read "Tom Brown's School Days at Rugby"?

Begin with capital letters words naming particular things or events of special importance; as,—

> *The Declaration of Independence*   *The Revolution*

Begin with capital letters the important words in the title of a book, of a newspaper, or of any other composition; as,—

> *Robinson Crusoe*   *Young People's Monthly*
> *My Trip to the Mountains*

IV

Mention in the following any name or title of God:—

1. The Lord is my shepherd.

2. Remember now thy Creator in the days of thy youth.

Begin with a capital letter any name or title of God; as,—

> *Lord   Creator   Father   the Supreme Being*

EXERCISE 1

Copy all the numbered sentences in this lesson, and tell why each capital letter is used.

EXERCISE 2

Copy the following stanza, and write it from memory: —

"All things bright and beautiful,
 All creatures great and small,
All things wise and wonderful,
 The Lord God made them all."

LESSON LXVIII

DICTATION EXERCISE

1. Alice is reading "Little Women."
2. All the Democrats voted against the bill.
3. The Natural Bridge is in Virginia.
4. The meeting was opened by Mayor Green.
5. We shall attend Grace Church.
6. How did you spend New Year's Day?
7. The President gave a public reception at the White House last Wednesday.
8. Why is the Declaration of Independence sometimes read on the Fourth of July?
9. The Pilgrims landed at Plymouth in December, 1620.
10. Howe'er it be, it seems to me,
  'Tis only noble to be good.
 Kind hearts are more than coronets,
  And simple faith than Norman blood.

        — TENNYSON.

C. Hayden

THE MAIDEN'S PETS

LESSON LXIX

A PICTURE LESSON

EXERCISE 1

Write a description of this picture.

Tell what person you see in the picture, describe the place where she is, and tell what she is doing.

EXERCISE 2

Write a story about this girl.

LESSON LXX

WORDS DERIVED FROM PROPER NAMES

Read the following sentences, and give the meaning of each word printed in italics : —

1. We speak the *English* language.
2. He works in a *Chinese* laundry.
3. The woman bought a *Japanese* fan.
4. The *American* flag is respected abroad.
5. These table-cloths are made of *Irish* linen.
6. Have you ever seen a *Mexican* pony?
7. The *Canadian* winters are enlivened by many outdoor sports.
8. The *German* band will play at the exercises.

9. Robert Burns was a *Scottish* poet.

10. Do not be too quick to follow *French* fashions.

The words in italics are derived from proper names.   With what kind of letter does each of those words begin ?

Begin with a capital letter every word derived from a proper name.

EXERCISE

Write sentences showing the correct use of the following words : —

English	Mexican	Italian	German
Russian	French	Irish	African
Roman	Norwegian	British	Chinese

LESSON LXXI

DICTATION EXERCISE

1. He bought a Swiss watch.
2. Who wrote " The Barefoot Boy " ?
3. The English sparrow is not a general favorite.
4. The schools were closed on Decoration Day.
5. Columbus made four voyages to the New World.
6. Who is your French teacher ?
7. The Russian winter is long and cold.
8. Horses were introduced into Mexico by the Spaniards.
9. Defoe's best known work is " Robinson Crusoe."
10. America has furnished to the world the character of Washington.

LESSON LXXII

REVIEW

EXERCISE 1

Make a statement about —

your book   a chain   a small boy   cold weather
the clock   the window   bright faces   kind words

How many parts has a statement? What does one of these parts name?

What does the other part tell?

What is a word used as a name called?

What is a name called that belongs to an individual person or thing? Give an example.

What is a name called that belongs to every person or thing of the same class? Give an example.

With what kind of letter should a proper name begin?

EXERCISE 2

Point out the nouns in these statements, and tell which are common names and which are proper names: —

1. The basket was filled with grapes.
2. Valuable minerals are found in the Rocky Mountains.
3. A fisherman hastened along the beach.
4. The robin is building a nest.
5.   Listen, my children, and you shall hear
       Of the midnight ride of Paul Revere.
6. I stood on the bridge at midnight.
7. My rambles soon led me to the church, which stood at a short distance from the village.

Tell why each capital letter is used in the following: —

1. This chair was made by the Shakers.

2. The tea-plant is cultivated in China.

3. Sir Walter Scott had a great affection for animals.

4. England is separated from France by the English Channel.

5. The Legislature will be in session on Monday evening.

6. The Governor has issued a Thanksgiving proclamation.

7. Charles is reading "The Old Curiosity Shop."

8. O Harry, see what I have found!

9. The chimney-piece is set round with Dutch tiles, representing scenes from Scripture.

10.   On Alpine heights the love of God is shed;
               He paints the morning red,
               The flowerets white and blue,
               And feeds them with his dew.
       On Alpine heights a loving Father dwells.

Write statements containing —

1. The name of a large city.

2. The name of a lake.

3. The name of a railroad.

4. The name of an express company.

5. The name of a hotel.

6. The name of a bank.

7. The name of a newspaper.

8. The name of a book.

LESSON LXXIII

COMPOSITION

EXERCISE 1

Read the following poem : —

THE FOUR SUNBEAMS

I

Four little sunbeams came earthward one day,
Shining and dancing along on their way,
    Resolved that their course should be blest.
" Let us try," they all whispered, "some kindness to do,
Not seek our own pleasuring all the day through,
    Then meet in the eve at the west."

II

One sunbeam ran in at a low cottage door,
And played "hide-and-seek" with a child on the floor,
    Till baby laughed loud in his glee,
And chased with delight his strange playmate so bright,
The little hands grasping in vain for the light
    That ever before them would flee.

III

One crept to the couch where an invalid lay,
And brought him a dream of the sweet summer day,
    Its bird-song and beauty and bloom ;
Till pain was forgotten and weary unrest,
And in fancy he roamed through the scenes he loved best,
    Far away from the dim, darkened room.

IV

One stole to the heart of a flower that was sad,
And loved and caressed her until she was glad
    And lifted her white face again ;
For love brings content to the lowliest lot,
And finds something sweet in the dreariest spot,
    And lightens all labor and pain.

V

And one, where a little blind girl sat alone,
Not sharing the mirth of her playfellows, shone
    On hands that were folded and pale,
And kissed the poor eyes that had never known sight,
That never would gaze on the beautiful light
    Till angels had lifted the veil.

VI

At last, when the shadows of evening were falling,
And the sun, their great father, his children was calling,
    Four sunbeams sped into the west.
All said, "We have found that in seeking the pleasure
Of others, we fill to the full our own measure," —
    Then softly they sank to their rest.
            —M. K. B., in *St. Nicholas.*

What did the four little sunbeams resolve to do?
What did the first sunbeam do?
How did the second sunbeam amuse an invalid?
What did the third sunbeam do to make a little flower happy?
How did the fourth sunbeam show the little blind girl that he
felt sorry for her?

What did all the little sunbeams say, when they went home at night?

Into how many stanzas is this poem divided? Tell what each stanza is about.

EXERCISE 2

Write in your own words the story of " The Four Sunbeams." Do not forget to begin every new sentence with a capital letter.

LESSON LXXIV

NAMES THAT MEAN MORE THAN ONE

What do you say when you speak of more than one —

clock?   book?   slate?   chair?

The form of a word used in speaking of one thing is called the **singular** form.

The form of a word used in speaking of more than one thing is called the **plural** form.

Write the words *clock, book, slate,* and *chair.*

Write the words that mean more than one *clock, book, slate,* and *chair.*

What did you add to each word, to make it mean more than one?

Add *s* to the singular of most nouns, to form the plural.

EXERCISE

Write sentences containing the plural forms of the following words :—

marble	basket	mile	hat
tree	pailful	hour	coat
bird	cupful	week	paper
car	spoonful	pencil	flag

LESSON LXXV

NAMES THAT MEAN MORE THAN ONE

What do you say when you speak of more than one —

dress?   box?   watch?   dish?

Write the words that mean more than one *dress, box, watch,* and *dish.*

What did you add to each word to make it mean more than one?

Pronounce the words above and notice the sound with which each word ends.

Nouns ending in a hissing sound like that of *s*, *x*, *sh*, *ch*, and *z*, form the plural by adding *es* to the singular; as, *gas, gases; tax, taxes; brush, brushes; watch, watches; topaz, topazes.*

EXERCISE

Write sentences containing the plural forms of these names: —

church	wish	class	match
glass	fox	peach	dish
dress	tax	house	watch
brush	grass	bush	ditch
bench	thrush	beech	hedge
hinge	horse	rose	breeze

Example. — There are five churches in the village.

LESSON LXXVI

ORAL COMPOSITION

EXERCISE 1

Read the following story:—

THE VAIN JACKDAW

Jupiter sent out a proclamation that on a certain day all of the birds should come together, when he himself would choose the most beautiful among them to be king.

The Jackdaw, knowing his own ugliness, yet wishing to make himself as attractive as possible, searched through the woods and fields for the feathers which had fallen from the wings of his companions. These he collected and stuck in all parts of his body.

When the appointed day arrived, the Jackdaw came with the others, in his many-feathered finery. Jupiter decided that the Jackdaw should be made king on account of the beauty of his plumage.

Upon this, the indignant birds whose feathers the Jackdaw was wearing flew to him, each plucking from him his own feathers. Thus the Jackdaw was again nothing but a Jackdaw.

EXERCISE 2

Tell in your own words the story of "The Vain Jackdaw."

LESSON LXXVII

NAMES THAT CHANGE *F* OR *FE* TO *VES*

leaf	loaf	knife
leaves	loaves	knives

Name the words in the foregoing list that mean one thing. Name the words that mean more than one.

Tell how the words are changed to make each mean more than one.

Some nouns ending in *f* or *fe* change *f* or *fe* to *ves* to form the plural.

EXERCISE

Write sentences containing the plural forms of the following names :—

shelf	half	calf	loaf
wolf	beef	life	sheaf
leaf	thief	wife	knife

Example. — The shelves were filled with books.

LESSON LXXVIII

REVIEW

EXERCISE 1

Read these statements, tell what is spoken of in each statement, and what is said about it:—

1. The birds were sitting on posts.
2. The farmer sold his calves.

3. A child bought two loaves of bread.
4. The taxes were paid.
5. George brought three pailfuls of water.
6. The leaves are green.
7. Two bridges were burned.
8. The trains were delayed.
9. Foxes have long bushy tails.
10. The thieves were sent to prison.

EXERCISE 2

Copy the numbered sentences in Exercise 1, and use singular nouns for the plural nouns.

Make such other changes in the sentences as may be necessary.

> **Example.** — The birds were sitting on posts.
> A bird was sitting on a post.

LESSON LXXIX

COMPOSITION

EXERCISE 1

Read this story : —

THE BOY AND THE WOLF

A boy, who kept a flock of sheep not far from a village, used to amuse himself by crying out, "Wolf! Wolf!" Then his neighbors would leave their work and run to help him, only to find that no wolf had been there. They were deceived in this way several times.

At last, a wolf really came. The boy went again to the men, and begged them, with many tears, to come to the rescue of his flock. But they thought that he was in sport as before, and paid no attention to his cries and tears. So he lost his sheep.

What is this story about ?[1] What was the boy doing? How did he amuse himself? What did his neighbors find when they came to help him?

What happened when a wolf really came?

What does this story teach?

EXERCISE 2

Write in your own words the story of "The Boy and the Wolf."

LESSON LXXX

PLURAL FORMS OF NAMES ENDING IN *Y*

Write the words —

      lady   city   ′cherry

With what letter does each of these words end?

What word means more than one lady? more than one city? more than one cherry?

Write the words that mean more than one *lady*, *city*, and *cherry*. How did you change each word, to make it mean more than one?

Some nouns ending in *y* change *y* to *ies*, to form the plural; as, *fly*, *flies*; *city*, *cities*; *army*, *armies*.

---

[1] To THE TEACHER. — Pupils should answer these questions and write the story without referring to their books.

Write the words—

day   key   boy

With what letter does each of these words end? What letter comes before y in *day*? in *key*? in *boy*?

Write the words that mean more than one *day*, *key*, and *boy*. What did you add to each word?

When a noun ends in y, if a, e, or o comes before the y, add s to the singular, to form the plural; as, *day, days; journey, journeys; toy, toys*.

EXERCISE 1

Copy the following words, and write opposite each name its plural form:—

lily	chimney	baby	body
daisy	berry	pony	city
fly	valley	donkey	duty
monkey	story	tidy	lady

Example.—Lily, lilies; valley, valleys.

EXERCISE 2

Write sentences containing the plural forms of the names above.

LESSON LXXXI

OTHER PLURAL FORMS

What word means more than one—

man?	tooth?	mouse?	foot?
goose?	ox?	woman?	child?

Some nouns form their plurals in irregular ways; as, *man, men; mouse, mice; child, children*.

1. The farmer counted his sheep.
2. One sheep was missing.
3. There are five deer in the park.
4. Have you ever seen a wild deer?

Read the sentences above. What word is used to denote one sheep? To denote more than one?

What is the singular form of the word *deer?* What is the plural form?

Some words have the same form in the singular and the plural; as, *sheep, deer, trout, cannon.*

EXERCISE

Write sentences containing the plural forms of these words : —

woman	ox	man	foot
child	tooth	mouse	goose

LESSON LXXXII

A PICTURE LESSON

EXERCISE 1

What persons are represented in this picture? Where are they? What do you think they are doing?

Describe the room in which they are working.

EXERCISE 2

Write a story about these little girls. Tell who they are and what they did one day.

Joseph Clark

DUMPLINGS

LESSON LXXXIII

REVIEW

When is a word said to be in the singular form?

When is a word said to be in the plural form?

How is the plural form of most nouns made? Mention f nouns that form the plural by adding *s* to the singular.

How do some nouns ending in a hissing sound like that of *s*, *sh*, etc. form the plural? Give five nouns that form the plural adding *es* to the singular.

How do some nouns ending in *f* or *fe* form the plural? G examples.

In how many ways do nouns ending in *y* form the plur Give examples of each way, and tell how the plural is form in each case.

Give five nouns that form the plural irregularly.

Give three nouns in which the singular and the plural form the same.

EXERCISE

(1) *Copy the following nouns, and opposite each no write its plural:* —

I

basket	Monday	roof	lasso
flower	gulf	chief	solo
boat	cuff	scarf	piano
turkey	day	cupful	spoonful
brother	chimney	valley	monkey
table	tree	fife	towel
chair	safe	hoof	picture

II

dish	*Miss* Smith[1]	hero	tomato
bench	potato	motto	mosquito

III

story	lily	army
city	enemy	navy

IV

leaf	knife	half	thief	life

V

woman	tooth	foot	*Mr.* Brown[2]

(2) *Write statements containing the plural forms of —*

ox	half	family	American	life
deer	chimney	shelf	German	city

(3) *Use in a question the plural form of —*

day	valley	leaf	journey
knife	path	lily	woman

(4) *Use in a command the plural form of —*

pony	baby	match	sponge
cherry	child	turkey	toy

---

[1] *Misses Smith* or *Miss Smiths.*
[2] *Messrs. Brown* or *Mr. Browns.*

LESSON LXXXIV

DICTATION EXERCISE

1. Butterflies have short lives.

2. Two families have already engaged rooms for the summer.

3. The thieves escaped.

4. The chimneys of three cities are in sight.

5. The hills and valleys are bright with autumn leaves.

6. Monkeys are found in the forests of Central America.

7. I bring fresh showers for the thirsting flowers.

8. Choose the timbers with greatest care.

9. The most extensive oyster fisheries in the world are carried on in Chesapeake Bay.

10. The State of Virginia is called the Old Dominion.

LESSON LXXXV

COMPOSITION

EXERCISE 1

Read the following :—

WHAT MAKES THE OCEAN SALT?

He who sails upon the sea must carry fresh water in his ship or perish with thirst, for he will find

"Water, water everywhere, nor any drop to drink."

What is the secret of the saltness of the sea? Its water was not always so. Every drop of it, at some time, came from the clouds, and was just as fresh as any rain-water. I will tell you the simple story. Raindrops patter upon hilltops and meadows everywhere. They sink into the soil and run over the rocks, all the time dissolving many things in their way; but they find more of salt than of any other one thing. Springs and rivulets gush from the hillside, rivers run from the highlands, and, swollen by others from the plains and valleys, at last pour their floods into the sea. Next comes in the work of the sunshine. The heat lifts the water, in the form of vapor, into the clouds, but it leaves the salt behind. Year after year this work goes on. Water, loaded with an easy burden of salt, travelling by easy stages to the sea, leaves its burden there, while it climbs the sunbeam up to the sky again to form the floating clouds. The clouds, wafted by the winds, fly away over the continents to drop upon forest and field their rattling rain, which must travel its oft-repeated journey to the sea again. In this way the ocean has received its salt.

—LE ROY C. COOLEY.

EXERCISE 2

Tell in your own words "What makes the Ocean Salt."

(1) Tell where the water of the sea comes from.

(2) Describe the course of the raindrops on their way to the sea, telling what they bear to the ocean, and what becomes of their burden.

(3) Tell how they reach the sky again.

(4) Tell what becomes of them there.

LESSON LXXXVI

WORDS THAT DENOTE POSSESSION

1. Henry has a sled.
2. Henry's sled is broken.

Who is spoken of in the first statement? What is said about Henry?

What is said about the sled in the second statement? What does the word *Henry's* show?

In the statements above, how many forms has the word *Henry?*

When a word is used to show to whom or to what something belongs, it is said to denote possession. The form of a word that denotes possession is called the **possessive form.**

1. The boy's hat is too large.
2. The doctor's horse ran away.
3. Here is a spider's web.

Whose hat is too large? Whose horse ran away? To what did the web belong?

What has been added to each of the words *boy, doctor,* and *spider,* to show that they denote possession?

Add the apostrophe (') and *s* to a singular noun, to form the possessive.

EXERCISE 1

Write sentences containing the following: —

Helen's letter   the day's work
a girl's hat   a squirrel's teeth

the boy's hand   a man's voice
a dog's bark   the grocer's wagon
a lady's glove   the lawyer's office

Example. — Helen's letter is interesting.

EXERCISE 2

Use the possessive forms of these words in sentences :—

| boy | bird | pony | father | Milly |
| child | merchant | mother | sister | Mr. Smith |

Example. — The boy's hat was too large.

LESSON LXXXVII

POSSESSIVE FORMS OF PLURAL NOUNS ENDING IN *S*

1. Boys' boots have thick soles.
2. The packages were left in the ladies' room.
3. The birds' nests are deserted.

Read the statements. Tell what each statement is about, and what is said about the thing spoken of.

Which words in these sentences denote possession?

Write the words *boys*, *ladies*, and *birds*. With what letter does each word end? What is added to each of these words in the foregoing sentences, to show that they denote possession?

Add the apostrophe (') to a plural noun ending in *s*, to form the possessive.

EXERCISE 1

Write sentences containing the possessive plural forms of these words : —

soldier	boy	pony	teacher	fox
sister	fly	horse	merchant	wolf

Example. — The soldiers' knapsacks are heavy.

EXERCISE 2

Change these sentences, so that the words in italics shall have the possessive form.

1. The voice of the *singer* was sweet.
2. The wings of the *bird* were black.
3. It was the house owned by your *father*.
4. I did not hear the name of the *lady*.
5. The back of a *toad* is rough.
6. Place these flowers in the room belonging to your *mother*.
7. Have you ever seen the track of a *fox?*
8. The arm of the *blacksmith* is strong.

Example. — The voice of the *singer* was sweet.
The *singer's* voice was sweet.

LESSON LXXXVIII

POSSESSIVE FORMS OF PLURAL NOUNS NOT ENDING IN S

1. Men's voices were heard.
2. Did you see the children's presents?

What does the first sentence do?   Whose voices were heard?

What does the second sentence do?   What is the use of the word *children's?*

Mention the words in these sentences that denote possession. What has been added to each of the words, to show that they denote possession?

Add the apostrophe (') and *s* to a plural noun not ending in *s*, to form the possessive.

EXERCISE 1

(1) *Copy the possessive forms below.   Tell which of the words mean one, and which mean more than one.*

(2) *Write sentences containing these possessive forms:*

boy's	sister's	ladies'
men's	boys'	teachers'
girls' ·	man's	women's
bee's	birds'	Herbert's

EXERCISE 2

Write sentences containing the possessive plural forms of the following words : —

doctor	woman	lady	child	pupil
horse	ox	brother	gentleman	dog

EXERCISE 3

Write the four forms of each of the nouns below : —

friend	father	neighbor	lawyer
sailor	mother	cousin	merchant
secretary	brother	lobster	ox

Example. — *Singular,* lady   lady's
           Plural,   ladies   ladies'

LESSON LXXXIX

A PICTURE LESSON

From G. Mader

THE TRIO

What does this picture represent? How many musicians are there, and upon what instruments are they playing? Where do you think they give pleasure by their playing?

Write a story about these little musicians.

LESSON XC

STUDY OF SELECTION

EXERCISE 1

Copy these lines: —

> When beechen buds begin to swell,
> . And woods the bluebird's warble know,
> The yellow violet's modest bell
>   Peeps from the last year's leaves below.
>
>   — BRYANT.

What flower is spoken of? What is meant by the violet's *bell?* What is the use of the word *yellow?* From under what leaves does the violet come?

When does the violet come? On what kind of tree do *beechen buds* grow? At what time in the year do beechen buds swell?

What bird is heard in the woods when the violet comes? What is meant by the bluebird's *warble?*

Which words in these lines have the possessive form? Tell how the possessive form is made in each case, and give the name of the thing possessed.

Tell in your own words when the yellow violet blossoms.

EXERCISE 2

Learn the stanza above, and then write it from memory.

LESSON XCI

DICTATION EXERCISE

1. Yonder is a robin's nest.
2. Call at the grocer's, and order some potatoes.

3. We have new styles in ladies' and children's suits.
4. Where is the yesterday's paper?
5. See whether the word is in Webster's Dictionary.
6. Edith's and Emma's exercises are neatly written.
7. Where is James's hat?
8. Charles's brother has gone to Montreal.

LESSON XCII

WORDS USED FOR NOUNS

1. "I will go," said Merton.
2. Robert, will you go to the river?
3. George stopped when he heard the train.
4. Nelly plays, but she does not sing.
5. Look at this fern.   It grew in the shade.

Whose words are repeated in the first sentence? Who is meant by *I?*

Who is addressed in the second sentence? Who is meant by *you?*

Who is spoken of in the third sentence? For what word is *he* used?

What is the first thing said about Nelly? What is the second thing said? For what word is *she* used?

How many statements are there in the last example? To what does *it* refer? Which words in these sentences are used instead of nouns?

A word used for a noun is a **pronoun**; as, *I, you, he, she, it.*

A pronoun that denotes the person speaking is said to be in **the first person.**

A pronoun that denotes a person spoken to is said to be in the **second person**.

A pronoun that denotes a person or a thing spoken of is said to be in the **third person**.

EXERCISE 1

Copy these sentences, and underline the pronouns : —

1. They are building a new house.
2. You knocked at the wrong door.
3. He wrote a letter to his brother.
4. We took our friends to see the painting.
5. He is older than your son.
6. The fishermen are mending their nets.
7. She laughed merrily.
8. Do you enjoy your work?
9. I looked for the book, but could not find it.
10. She invited us to ride with her.
11. Do with all your might whatever you have to do, without thinking of the future.

EXERCISE 2

Write two statements about each person or thing named below. In the first statement use the name of the person or thing, and in the second statement use a pronoun referring to that name : —

camel	horse	cotton	Emma
Ralph	man	coal	Rover

Example. — The camel is used in crossing the desert. It can go without water for a week.

LESSON XCIII

SELECTION TO BE MEMORIZED

Read the following poem, and commit it to memory: —

THE SEA

The sea! the sea! the open sea!
The blue, the fresh, the ever free!
Without a mark, without a bound,
It runneth the earth's wide regions round;
It plays with the clouds; it mocks the skies;
Or like a cradled creature lies.

I'm on the sea! I'm on the sea!
I am where I would ever be;
With the blue above, and the blue below,
And silence wheresoe'er I go;
If a storm should come and awake the deep,
What matter? *I* shall ride and sleep.

I love, O, *how* I love to ride
On the fierce, foaming, bursting tide,
When every mad wave drowns the moon,
Or whistles aloft his tempest tune,
And tells how goeth the world below,
And why the sou'west blasts do blow.

I never was on the dull, tame shore,
But I loved the great sea more and more,
And backwards flew to her billowy breast,

Like a bird that seeketh its mother's nest;
And a mother she *was*, and *is*, to me;
For I was born on the open sea!

The waves were white, and red the morn,
In the noisy hour when I was born;
And the whale it whistled, the porpoise rolled,
And the dolphins bared their backs of gold;
And never was heard such an outcry wild
As welcomed to life the ocean-child!

I've lived since then, in calm and strife,
Full fifty summers, a sailor's life,
With wealth to spend and a power to range,
But never have sought nor sighed for change;
And Death, whenever he comes to me,
Shall come on the wild, unbounded sea!

—BRYAN WALLER PROCTER (BARRY CORNWALL).

LESSON XCIV

ORAL COMPOSITION

EXERCISE 1

Read the following story:—

PROSERPINE[1]

One day, Proserpine, the daughter of Ceres,[2] was playing with other children on the bank of a lake. They were gathering the violets that grew in the fields, and were plaiting them into crowns for their hair.

---

[1] Proserpine (*prŏs'-er-pĭn*). [2] Ceres (*sē'-rēz*).

All at once Proserpine saw the most beautiful flower imaginable growing at some distance from the spot where they were playing. It grew up high above the other flowers in the meadow, and was of a beautiful glowing crimson color. She ran to get it, and as she came near, she saw that it had as many as a hundred fragrant lily-shaped blossoms all clustering around one stem. It was the most splendid flower! But she had wandered far away from the other children without being aware of it.

Just as she was stretching out her hand to pick the wonderful flowers she heard a rumbling sound, which seemed to come from under the ground, and all at once the sunshine did not seem so bright as it had before. Proserpine was frightened, and would have liked to run back where the other children were, but it did seem too bad to leave such a splendid flower. While she stood there, not quite knowing what to do, the earth suddenly opened, and she saw a yawning black hole, close to her side.

The rumbling sound grew louder — Proserpine was now too frightened to run away — and a chariot drawn by four black horses came whirling up out of the black hole and stopped suddenly in front of Proserpine. A gloomy-looking man sprang from it, caught her up in his arms, returned to the chariot, and went whirling away with her, Proserpine screaming loudly for her mother, and the flowers falling from her torn apron all the way.

Not long after, the children who had been playing with Proserpine came to look for her. But they only found a few violets that had fallen from her apron. There was nothing to be seen of the black hole. They had to go home and tell her mother, Ceres, that Proserpine was lost.

Ceres was quite broken-hearted at this news. But with-out loss of time she lighted a torch, for it was now dark, and went out to look for her daughter.

After she had wandered about the world for ten days, asking every one she met if they had seen her daughter, she bethought her to ask Helios, the sun-god, who sees everything. He told her at once that Pluto, the king of the lower world, had carried off Proserpine.

When she heard this Ceres was very angry, and in her anger she laid a curse on the fruits of the earth — for Ceres was the earth-mother.

Then nothing could grow out of the earth. There was no wheat or other grain to be made into bread for the people, the trees could bear no fruit, and there were no flowers to brighten the fields. Even the grass could not grow, and the cattle must go hungry. Then there was famine and plague.

Jupiter, the father of the gods, looked down from his throne and saw that all the people on the earth would die unless Ceres took her curse away; and he sent Mercury down to the lower world to bring Proserpine back to her mother.

But before King Pluto would let Proserpine go, he gave her a pomegranate to eat, and although she ate only a few of the seeds, yet because she had eaten those few seeds she was obliged to stay for six months of every year with

King Pluto, and could only return to her mother during the other six months of the year.

While Proserpine is on the earth, the fields are clothed with grass, flowers bloom, fruits ripen, and all nature pulses with life; but when Proserpine returns to the lower world again, the earth is cold and bare and lifeless; for Ceres, the earth-mother, mourns for her daughter.

EXERCISE 2

Tell in your own words the story of "Proserpine."

LESSON XCV

WORDS THAT DESCRIBE

1. This bird has black wings.
2. An old sword hung above the door.
3. The boy carried a large basket.

Read the first statement. What is the use of the word *black*.

What is the second statement about? What is the use of the word *old?*

What does the third statement tell? What word limits the meaning of the noun *boy* to some particular boy?

What words in the sentences above are used to describe something or to limit the meaning of nouns?

A word that limits the application or adds to the meaning of another word is said to **modify** that word, and is called a **modifier**; as, *kind* words; *this* week; *the* boy.

A word used to modify the meaning of a noun or pronoun is an **adjective**; as, The sky is *blue*. She is *happy*.

Mention adjectives that can be used to describe —

| a knife | an apple | a hat |
| a house | a book | a cat |

EXERCISE 1

Use each of the following words in a sentence, to describe something : —

tall	busy	large	obedient
amusing	straight	cool	sunny
true	slender	smiling	old

Example. — A tall boy held the horse.

EXERCISE 2

Write sentences containing the following words used as adjectives : —

| each | few | these | both |
| this | many | some | no |

Example. — Each boy carried a flag.

LESSON XCVI

COMPOSITION

DESCRIPTION OF LOST ARTICLE

Suppose that you have lost something. Describe the lost article. Be careful to use words that will show exactly what thing is meant.

Describe a lost —

| knife | hat | horse |
| purse | dog | cow |

Example. — Lost. — A *small pocket* knife with a *pearl* handle. It has *two* blades, one *long* and *broad*, the other *short* and *slender*. The *small* blade has a *broken* point.

LESSON XCVII

STUDY OF SELECTION

[The following lines are taken from the poem called "The Children's Hour." The poet is describing his own children on their way to his study.]

> I hear in the chamber above me
>   The patter of little feet,
> The sound of a door that is opened,
>   And voices soft and sweet.
>
> From my study, I see in the lamplight,
>   Descending the broad hall stair,
> Grave Alice and laughing Allegra [1]
>   And Edith with golden hair.
>
> — LONGFELLOW.

Who wrote these lines? Read the first stanza.

What is the first thing that the poet says? *Where* does **he** hear something? Who is meant by *me*?

[1] Allegra (*al-lā'gra*).

What word joins the noun *chamber* and the verb *hear*? What word shows the relation between the chamber and the poet?

What is the first thing that the poet hears? Of what does he hear the patter? Do children run or walk when their feet patter? What is the second thing that the poet hears? What is the third thing? What words describe the voices?

Read the second stanza. From what place does the writer see something? In what light does he see something? What does he see? What are they doing?

What does *descending* mean? What does the word *hall* show? What is the use of *broad*?

What kind of girl was Alice? What is the meaning of *grave*? What word describes Allegra? What word describes Edith? Do they describe something about her appearance or her character?

Tell in your own words what the poet heard. Tell what he saw.

WRITTEN EXERCISES

Copy the two stanzas above, and commit them to memory. Copy the following sentences, writing other words of similar meaning in place of the words in Italics: —

1. I hear the *patter* of *little* feet.
2. The voices are *soft*.
3. The children are *descending* the stairs.
4. The stair is *broad*.
5. Alice is *grave*.
6. Edith has *golden* hair.
7. What *sound* did you hear?
8. They are sitting in the *study*.
9. I *see* three children.

LESSON XCVIII

COMPOSITION

DESCRIPTION OF OUR FLAG

Write a description of the national flag of the United States. Tell its shape and color, and name its different parts. Tell which parts are red, which white, and which blue, and show how the different parts are placed. State the number of stripes, and tell why that number is used. Give the number of stars, and tell what each represents.

> "'Tis the star spangled banner! oh, long may it wave
> O'er the land of the free, and the home of the brave!"

LESSON XCIX

WORDS THAT POINT OUT

1. This orange is sweet.
2. These oranges are sweet.
3. Did you see that bird?
4. It flew over those trees.

Read the first sentence. For what is *this* used?
What word in the second statement shows which oranges are meant?
What does the third sentence do? What is the use of *that?*
Where did the bird fly? What is the use of *those?*
In the sentences above what word is used to point out one thing near by? What word is used to point out two or more things near by?
What word is used to point out one thing at a distance? What word is used to point out two or more things at a distance?

Use *this* to point out one thing near by.
Use *these* to point out two or more things near by.
Use *that* to point out one thing at a distance.
Use *those* to point out two or more things at a distance.

EXERCISE

Copy the following sentences, using these *in place of* this, *and* those *in place of* that. *Make such other changes as may be necessary:* —

1. This knife is sharp.
2. Look at that chimney.
3. Is this glove yours?
4. That horse has a heavy load.
5. Did you find that key?
6. That star is bright.
7. Jack Frost drew this picture.
8. Have you read that magazine?
9. This leaf has a notched edge.

Example. — These knives are sharp.

LESSON Ċ

THE, AND *AN* OR *A*

1. A boy stood by the window.
2. The boy had light hair.
3. An apple fell from the tree.
4. The apple was large.

Read the sentences. Was it any particular boy that stood by the window? What boy had light hair?

Are we told what apple fell from the tree? What apple is spoken of in the fourth sentence? If you should say, " Bring me *an* apple," would you mean any apple in particular? What would you mean if you should say, " Bring me *the* apple "?

The is used when some particular thing is meant.
An or *a* is used when no particular thing is meant.

1. A birch tree has smooth bark.
2. An apple lay on the table.
3. We passed an old house.
4. The boys are learning a new game.

What kind of tree is spoken of in the first sentence? What is the second sentence about? Give the first sound in the word *birch ;* in the word *apple.* What word is used before birch? What one before apple?

What word describes *house ?* What word describes *game ?* Give the first sound in the word *old.* What word is used before *old ?* Give the first sound in the word *new.* What word is used before *new ?*

Which of the words *birch, apple, old,* and *new* begin with vowel[1] sounds? What word is used before each of those words? What word is used before the other words?

An is used before words beginning with vowel sounds ; *a* is used before other words.

---

[1] The sounds of the letters *a, e, i, o,* and *u* are vowel sounds ; the sounds of the other letters are consonant sounds.

EXERCISE 1

Pronounce these words, and use an before the words beginning with vowel sounds and a before the other words:—

orange	owl	axe	oak	wonder
inch	unit	honor	ewe	one
boat	hour	yoke	maple	apple
year	horn	ear	island	egg

Examples.—An orange ; a boat.

NOTE.—Always notice the first sound of a word, not its first letter. We say *an* hour (*h* is silent), many *a* one (*one* begins with the consonant sound of *w*), *a* useful article (*useful* begins with the consonant sound of *y*).

EXERCISE 2

Copy the following sentences, and fill the blanks with an or a:—

1. The window is shaded by —— large tree.
2. Please lend me —— pencil.
3. —— old man entered the door.
4. He wore —— new coat.
5. You may stay —— hour.
6. He was riding in —— carriage.
7. Can you catch —— ball?
8. —— narrow path led to the river.
9. They took —— early train.
10. Do not make —— unkind remark.
11. —— boat was fastened to the wharf.
12. Did you ever see —— owl?

LESSON CI

COMPOSITION

A WALK

Write about some walk that you have taken.

What kind of day was it when you took your walk?

If your walk was in the city, did you go through quiet or noisy streets? What kind of carriages passed you? What did you see in the windows? What kind of men, women, and children did you meet? What else did you see?

If your walk was in the country, did you walk in the road or in the fields? What was growing in the fields? What flowers did you see? What trees were in sight? What animals did you see, and what were they doing?

LESSON CII

REVIEW

EXERCISE 1

Give a word that will tell the color of —

    the sky   the grass   the snow

What word may be used to tell —

    the shape of an orange?   the size of an orange?
    the taste of an orange?   the number of oranges?

Name a word that may be used to point out one thing near by; one thing at a distance.

Name a word that may be used to point out two or more things near by; two or more things at a distance.

For what is *the* used? Give an example.

For what is *an* or *a* used? When should we use *an* ? When should we use *a* ?

EXERCISE 2

Use each of these words in a sentence, to describe or point out something : —

.interesting	an	the	sleepy
smooth	red	heavy	thirsty
this	these	those	large
cold	honest	small	kind
pretty	tired	long	pleasant

Example. — I am reading an interesting book.

LESSON CIII

DICTATION EXERCISE

1. All caterpillars shed their skins several times before they reach their full growth.

2. Silkworms feed upon the leaves of the mulberry tree.

3. The silkworm spins a cocoon of fine silk. The cocoon is about the size of a robin's egg.

4. The silkworm was known in China more than four thousand years ago. It has been carried from China to many other countries. It is now raised in some parts of the United States.

LESSON CIV

WORDS THAT ASSERT

Tell some of the things that birds do. What do dogs do? What do cats do? What do bees do?

1. Lions roar.
2. Soldiers march.
3. Rabbits have long ears.
4. The apple is red.

What word tells what lions do? What word tells what soldiers do?

What is said about rabbits? Read the third sentence, leaving out the word *have*, and see if the remaining words tell anything about the rabbits.

What is told about the apple? What is the use of the word *red?* If you take away *is*, do the remaining words form a sentence? Why not?

In every sentence, some word is used to tell or assert.

A word that asserts is a **verb**; as, The sun *shines*.

The word that denotes the person or thing about which the assertion is made is called the **subject** of the verb; as, The *sun* shines.

EXERCISE 1

Point out each verb in the following sentences, and name its subject: —

1. Plants need sunshine.
2. The dog welcomed his master.
3. The bluebird comes in early spring.
4. A small stream flows through the field.

5. We gathered pebbles on the beach.
6. The parrot's name is Polly.
7. Two men stepped from the carriage.
8. He opened the gate.
9. We entered the city at ten o'clock.
10. The hunter raised his gun.

EXERCISE 2

Write sentences, using each of the following as verbs : —

rises	have	forgot	walked
looked	has	flew	built
wrote	is	received	grows
was	were	opened	live

EXERCISE 3

Write sentences, using each of the following words as the subject of a verb. Underline the verbs : —

artist	they	door
soldier	clock	carriage
boy	slippers	flowers
he	carpenters	clouds

LESSON CV

TRANSITIVE AND INTRANSITIVE VERBS

1. The wind blows.
2. The bell rang.
3. Henry threw the ball.
4. The kitten caught a mouse.

Mention the verb in each sentence, and name its subject.

What is asserted of Henry?   Which word tells what Henry threw ?

Which word tells what the kitten caught, or denotes the thing receiving the action expressed by the verb?

The noun or pronoun that denotes the person or thing receiving the action expressed by a verb is called the **object of the verb**.   Some verbs require objects to complete their meaning.

A verb that requires an object is a **transitive verb**.

A verb that does not require an object is an **intransitive verb**.

EXERCISE

Copy these sentences.   Underline the verbs, the subjects of the verbs, and the objects of the transitive verbs :—

1. The cat caught a mouse.
2. John lost his ticket.
3. Grocers sell butter.
4. The teacher rang the bell.
5. The wheel moved.
6. Birds build nests.
7. The horse broke his halter.
8. Artists paint pictures.
9. Newsboys sell papers.
10. She sat by the table.
11. Grace brought the paper.
12. Walter gathered the pears.
13. The captain left the boat.
14. I met a little cottage girl.

LESSON CVI

SINGULAR AND PLURAL FORMS OF VERBS

1. The camel bears heavy burdens.
2. Camels bear heavy burdens.
3. The boat moves slowly.
4. The boats move slowly.

Mention the verb in each sentence and name its subject.

Which verbs have singular subjects?   Which have plural subjects? How do the verbs used with the singular subjects differ in form from those used with the plural subjects?

The form of a verb used with a singular subject is called the **singular form.**

The form of a verb used with a plural subject is called the **plural form.**

Most verbs used with singular subjects in the third person add *s* or *es*, to form the singular; as, *walk, walks; go, goes*.

A few verbs have special forms for singular and plural subjects; as, —

He *is* here.	He *was* there.
They *are* here.	They *were* there..

He *has* the book.
They *have* the book.

EXERCISE 1

Point out the singular and the plural forms of the verbs in the following sentences, and tell why each form is used : —

1. The stockings hang by the chimney.
2. The shadows dance upon the wall.
3. The mountains are covered with snow.
4. The birds have gone to rest.
5. This stream flows rapidly.
6. The exercises begin at eight o'clock.
7. The house stands on the side of a hill.
8. A sycamore grows by the door.

9. His voice is soft and gentle.
10. The ships were loaded with tea.
11. These timbers are valuable.
12. The spring comes slowly up this way.
13.   The walls are high, and the shores are steep,
      And the stream is strong, and the water deep.
14. Too many cooks spoil the broth.
15. He goes on Sunday to the church.

EXERCISE 2

Write sentences containing the following words used as verbs : —

live	· comes	rides	are	were
tells	make	hears	moves	go
builds	come	has	was	goes

EXERCISE 3

Write sentences containing the following, used correctly as subjects of singular verbs : —

September	wind	chair
window	path	forest
nephew	night	street

EXERCISE 4

Write sentences containing the following, used correctly as subjects of plural verbs : —

caterpillars	trees	stars
houses	swallows	merchants
railroads	brothers	Americans

LESSON CVII

STUDY OF A DESCRIPTION

HOW FLIES WALK

You have often seen a fly walking on the ceiling or running up a smooth pane of glass, and have wondered how it could hold on.

By examining the foot of a fly with a powerful microscope, it has been found that a fly's foot is made up of two little pads, upon which grow very fine short hairs. These hairs are so very fine that there are more than a thousand on each foot-pad. The hairs are hollow, with trumpet-shaped mouths. Back of the pad is a little bag filled with liquid glue. When the fly steps, it presses the liquid through these hollow hairs out of the little mouths. The moment the glue reaches the air it hardens. Thus we see that at every step the fly takes, it glues itself to the surface. When the fly lifts its foot, it draws it up gently in a slanting direction, just as you might remove a moist postage-stamp, by beginning at one corner and gently drawing it back.

EXERCISE 1

Of what two parts is a fly's foot made up? How was this found out? What grow on each foot-pad? Describe the hairs. Name a flower that is *trumpet-shaped*. What is back of the pad? What takes place each time that the fly steps? How does the fly lift its foot?

EXERCISE 2

*Write sentences illustrating the correct use of the follow-
ing words :—*

ceiling	smooth	examine	powerful
microscope	hollow	trumpet	liquid
glue	surface	slanting	moist

EXERCISE 3

Tell in your own words "How Flies Walk."

1. Give a description of a fly's foot.
2. Tell what takes place when the fly steps.

LESSON CVIII

ORAL COMPOSITION

EXERCISE 1

Read the following story :—

ORPHEUS AND EURYDICE[1]

Orpheus, the son of Apollo, could play so sweetly on his
lyre, that all kinds of wild beasts — lions and tigers and
wolves, — and birds — little singing birds, and great hawks
and eagles, — and even the trees and the rocks gathered
around him to listen.

One day, his wife, Eurydice, was bitten by a serpent.
Then she had to leave Orpheus and go down into the
dark lower world, where Pluto was king and Proserpine
queen.

[1] Orpheus (*or'-fĭ-ŭs*).   Eurydice (*yū-rĭd'-ĭs-ē*).

Orpheus loved Eurydice so well that he could not bear to stay on the earth without her, so he followed her down into the lower world, playing on his lyre all the way. He played so sadly and so sweetly before Pluto and Proserpine, that Pluto gave his permission for Eurydice to return to the earth, on one condition. This was, that Orpheus should not look back to see if Eurydice was coming.

So they started, Orpheus playing on his lyre, and Eurydice following. They had almost reached the familiar upper world, and could see the sun rising over the sea, when Orpheus looked back, thus breaking his promise to Pluto. He only saw Eurydice fading away, and reaching out her arms to him in farewell, for now she must return to the lower world.

Then Orpheus sat down on the bank of the river Styx, and played on his lyre, and sang sad music, while the tears fell from his eyes, till he had wept and sung his life away. Then he went to live with Eurydice in the lower world, and they were never separated any more.

EXERCISE 2

Tell in your own words the story of "Orpheus and Eurydice."

LESSON CIX

WORDS THAT SHOW *HOW*

1. He spoke kindly.
2. The boat moved slowly.
3. Charles writes well.
4. The wind blows gently.

Read the first sentence. What is the use of *kindly?*

What is the second statement about? What word asserts something of the *boat?* What is the use of the word *slowly?*

What word asserts an action of *Charles?* What is the use of the word *well?*

What word asserts something of the *wind?* What does *gently* show?

In the foregoing sentences, which words are used with verbs to modify their meanings? What do these words show?

EXERCISE 1

Read the following sentences, supplying words that will tell how —

1. The snow falls.
2. The river runs.
3. The children laughed.
4. The man worked.
5. Anna sang.
6. The soldiers marched.
7. The tired child sleeps.
8. The boy waited.
9. The cricket chirps.
10. The gloves were mended.

EXERCISE 2

Copy the following sentences, underline the verbs, and fill the blanks with words showing how the actions are performed: —

1. The man walks ——.
2. Ruth reads ——.
3. The bell rings ——.
4. Horace crossed the street ——.
5. The snow falls ——.
6. She speaks —— and ——.
7. The door swings ——.

8. The children play ——
9. Laura thinks ——.
10. Snails move ——.
11. The boy writes ——.

EXERCISE 3

Use each of the following words in a sentence, to show **how** *some action is performed:* —

easily	quickly	quietly
generously	plainly	fast
patiently	carefully	noisily
distinctly	brightly	neatly
pleasantly	merrily	carelessly

LESSON CX

WORDS THAT SHOW *WHEN*

1. I wrote four letters yesterday.
2. Alice rides often.
3. The magazine is published monthly.
4. He seldom spoke of the war.

What word in the first sentence asserts an action? What is the use of the word *yesterday?*

What word asserts something of *Alice?* What does *often* do?

What is the third statement about? What word shows *how often* the magazine is published?

What word asserts something of *he?* What is the use of *seldom?*

Name the words in the sentences above that show *when* or *how often* actions were performed?

EXERCISE 1

Copy the following sentences, and underline the words th
show when :—

1. They went home early.
2. I saw the picture yesterday.
3. The paper came to-day.
4. Always speak the truth.
5. I will go presently.
6. Cross the bridge, then follow the crowd.
7. Never be discouraged.

EXERCISE 2

Use the following words in sentences, to show when som
thing was done.   Underline the verbs :—

often	soon	never	afterward	always
now	yesterday	quickly	early	late

LESSON CXI

WORDS THAT SHOW *WHERE*

1. The man stood here.
2. He stepped forward.
3. Charles threw the ball down.

In the sentences above what does the word *here* show? the wo
forward? the word *down?*

Give a sentence in which the meaning of the verb is modified
a word showing *how*. Give one in which the meaning of the ve
is modified by a word showing *when*.

A word that modifies the meaning of a verb is an adverb.

Sometimes an adverb is used to modify the meaning of an adjective ; as, —

This pencil is *too* short.

Sometimes an adverb is used to modify the meaning of another adverb ; as, —

He speaks *very* rapidly.

EXERCISE 1

Copy the following statements, adding words to show where : —

1. The tree stood.
2. The boy jumped.
3. The train moved.
4. The man looked.
5. We see the stars.
6. He threw the box.
7. The family moved.
8. The children ran.

EXERCISE 2

Use these words in sentences, to modify verbs, adjectives, or other adverbs : —

away	neatly	very	back	almost
backward	swiftly	here	there	down

LESSON CXII

COMPOSITION

Tell as clearly as you can how to do any one of the following things : —

How to Pop Corn.
How to Make Molasses Candy.
How to Make a Bed.
How to Ride a Bicycle.

How to Harness a Horse.
How to Make a Kite.
How to Catch a Crab.
How to Row a Boat.

HOW TO POP CORN

What kind of corn is best for popping? How do you prepare it? How much corn do you put into the corn-popper at a time? Where do you hold the corn-popper? Do you hold it still or keep it moving? Why? How will the corn look when it is done?

LESSON CXIII

USE OF NEGATIVES

Tell which of these sentences affirm, and which deny : —

The articles will be found.
The articles will never be found.

These grapes are ripe.
These grapes are not ripe.

He knows something about the matter.
He knows little about the matter.
He does not know anything about the matter.

I told one person.
I never told you that.
I did not tell anybody.

Our climate is warmer than theirs.
Our climate is not warm.

A sentence that affirms is called **affirmative**, and one that denies is called **negative**.

Which of the foregoing sentences are affirmative? Which are negative?

A word that denies is called a **negative**.

Name the negatives in the sentences above.

Do not use two negatives in the same sentence, unless you wish to express an affirmation.

EXERCISE 1

Change these sentences, making each express a meaning opposite to the meaning given: —

1. Your mail has come.
2. The boy is better.
3. He will pay something for the use of the carriage.
4. I did not give him anything.
5. Don't tell anybody.
6. Speak to the child.
7. It will do no good.
8. He did not put anything into the box.
9. The nurse followed the directions given.
10. They said something to the owner of the boat.
11. He will arrive before night.
12. The matter was not explained.
13. I saw nothing like this.
14. I did not learn anything about the accident.
15. They never found the watch.

Example. — Your mail has not come.

LESSON CXIV

A PICTURE LESSON

J. Denneulin

THE DEPARTURE

EXERCISE 1

Why are these men, women, and children assembled on the beach? Who do you think has gone away in the ship? Why is the dog so interested?

What kind of shoes do these people wear? What does that tell you about their home? How many baskets do you see? What are they for?

EXERCISE 2

Write the story that the picture tells you.

LESSON CXV

REVIEW

EXERCISE 1

What is a proper name?

With what kind of letter should a proper name begin?

In each of the following sentences tell whether the italicized word is a noun or a verb. Give reasons for your statements: —

1. Your *watch* is too slow.
2. Sailors *watch* the sky.
3. The *rose* is fragrant.
4. Edith *rose* from the chair.
5. The house is built on a *rock*.
6. The waves *rock* the vessel.

EXERCISE 2

Give a sentence containing an adjective used to point out something; an adjective used to describe something; an adverb used to show how something is done.

Read these sentences and tell whether the italicized words are adjectives or adverbs. Give reasons: —

1. We came on the *fast* train.
2. Do not talk so *fast*.
3. The woman has a *patient* face.
4. He performed the task *patiently*.
5. We had a *pleasant* ride.
6. Speak *pleasantly*.

EXERCISE 3

Write sentences containing the following words used as nouns : —

ride	ring	plant	saw	plough
iron	roof	carpet	light	rose

EXERCISE 4

Write sentences containing the following words used as verbs : —

ride	carpet	plant	plough	light
iron	ring	saw	walk	speak

EXERCISE 5

Write sentences containing the following words used as adjectives : —

kind	white	strange	bright	soft
tall	deep	rapid	light	shrill

EXERCISE 6

Write sentences containing the following words used as adverbs : —

well	fast	often	here	gently
now	far	slowly	kindly	lightly

EXERCISE 7

Write sentences containing the following words used as the subjects of verbs : —

clock	boat	fern	robin	dog
house	basket	bell	wren	horse

LESSON CXVI

WORDS THAT SHOW RELATION

In the following sentences find the words that join nouns or pronouns to other words : —

    1. Fishes live in water.

    2. Raindrops come from the clouds.

    3. Look at them.

A word used with a noun or pronoun to show its relation to some other word in the sentence is a *preposition.*

The noun or pronoun used with a preposition in this manner is called its **object.**

EXERCISE 1

Copy the following sentences, filling the blanks with prepositions : —

    1. The stream runs —— the bridge.

    2. The leaves fall —— the trees.

    3. Currants grow —— bushes.

    4. The lawn is covered —— grass.

    5. A bird —— the hand is worth two —— the bush.

    6. The clock stands —— the shelf.

    7. The river flows —— the sea.

    8. No one looked —— him.

EXERCISE 2

Copy the following sentences, and draw lines under the prepositions and under the objects of the prepositions : —

    1. The man walked across the bridge.

    2. One oar fell into the water.

3. The child ran to its mother.
4. Who went with her?
5. My hat is on the table.
6. The cherries on this tree are ripe.
7. They passed through the city.
8. His coat was lined with silk.

LESSON CXVII

STUDY OF SELECTION

ROBERT OF LINCOLN

I

Merrily swinging on brier and weed,
  Near to the nest of his little dame,
Over the mountain-side or mead,
  Robert of Lincoln is telling his name:
      Bob-o'-link, bob-o'-link,
      Spink, spank, spink;
  Snug and safe is that nest of ours,
  Hidden among the summer flowers.
      Chee, chee, chee.

II

Robert of Lincoln is gayly drest,
  Wearing a bright black wedding coat;
White are his shoulders and white his crest,
  Hear him call in his merry note:
      Bob-o'-link, bob-o'-link,
      Spink, spank, spink;

Look, what a nice new coat is mine,
Sure there was never a bird so fine.
Chee, chee, chee.

III

Robert of Lincoln's Quaker wife,
Pretty and quiet, with plain brown wings,
Passing at home a patient life,
Broods in the grass while her husband sings:
Bob-o'-link, bob-o'-link,
Spink, spank, spink;
Brood, kind creature; you need not fear
Thieves and robbers while I am here.
Chee, chee, chee.

IV

Modest and shy as a nun is she;
One weak chirp is her only note.
Braggart and prince of braggarts is he,
Pouring boasts from his little throat:
Bob-o'-link, bob-o'-link,
Spink, spank, spink;
Never was I afraid of man;
Catch me, cowardly knaves, if you can.
Chee, chee, chee.

V

Six white eggs on a bed of hay,
Flecked with purple, a pretty sight!

There as the mother sits all day,
  Robert is singing with all his might:
    Bob-o'-link, bob-o'-link,
    Spink, spank, spink;
  Nice good wife, that never goes out,
  Keeping house while I frolic about.
        Chee, chee, chee.

VI

Soon as the little ones chip the shell,
  Six wide mouths are open for food;
Robert of Lincoln bestirs him well,
  Gathering seeds for the hungry brood.
    Bob-o'-link, bob-o'-link,
    Spink, spank, spink;
  This new life is likely to be
  Hard for a gay young fellow like me.
        Chee, chee, chee.

VII

Robert of Lincoln at length is made
  Sober with work, and silent with care;
Off is his holiday garment laid,
  Half-forgotten that merry air, —
    Bob-o'-link, bob-o'-link,
    Spink, spank, spink;
  Nobody knows but my mate and I
  Where our nest and our nestlings lie.
        Chee, chee, chee.

VIII

Summer wanes: the children are grown;
Fun and frolic no more he knows;
Robert of Lincoln's a humdrum crone;
Off he flies, and we sing as he goes:
  Bob-o'-link, bob-o'-link,
  Spink, spank, spink;
When you can pipe that merry old strain,
Robert of Lincoln, come back again.
    Chee, chee, chee.
                              —WILLIAM CULLEN BRYANT.

What is the poem about?

Read the first stanza. Where was Robert of Lincoln? What was he doing? What word would be used in prose instead of *mead?* What do the fifth and sixth lines tell? What are the two following lines about? What is meant by the nest's being *snug?* What is meant by its being *safe?* What are the closing words of the song?

Read the second stanza. What does the first line tell? What do the second and third lines do? What is meant by *his crest?* What is the hearer requested to do in the fourth line? What is the song about?

Read the third stanza. What are the first four lines about? Why is Robert's wife called a *Quaker* wife? Which words describe her appearance? What does the wife do? Where does she brood? What does her husband sing to her?

Read the fourth stanza. What are contrasted in the first four lines? To what is the wife compared? What is said about her singing? What is the husband called? What are his words?

Read the fifth stanza. How many eggs are spoken of? Of what color were they? What did the mother do all day? What did Robert do?

Read the sixth stanza. What is the meaning of *chip?* What happened when the shells were chipped? What did Robert do then? What was his song now?

Read the seventh stanza. How did the work and care affect Robert? What is meant by *laying off his holiday garment?*

Ans. Changing his color.

What was half-forgotten? What is meant by *mate* in the seventh line? By *nestlings* in the eighth line?

Read the last stanza. What is the first statement? What is the meaning of *wanes?* What is the second statement? The third? To what does *he* refer in the second line? What is Robert called in the third line? Where does he go? When shall we welcome him back?

EXERCISE 1

Copy the first two stanzas of this poem, and commit them to memory.

EXERCISE 2

Write about "Robert of Lincoln."

1. Describe Robert of Lincoln's appearance, tell where he sings, and what he says in his song.
2. Describe his wife, and tell what she does.
3. Tell about Robert's work, and about his departure.
4. Tell what you know about the life of the bobolink.

LESSON CXVIII

NOMINATIVE FORMS OF PRONOUNS

1. We walked to the beach.
2. She joined the children.
3. They are gathering pebbles.

What word makes the assertion in the first sentence? What word is the subject of the verb *walked?*

Who joined the children? What is the subject of *joined?*

What does the third sentence tell? What is the subject of the verb?

The words *I, he, she, we,* and *they* take the place of nouns used as the subjects of verbs.

The form of a pronoun that is used as the subject of a verb is the *nominative form.*

EXERCISE

Copy the following sentences, filling the blanks with the nominative forms, **I, he, she, we,** *or* **they.** *In sentences like these, the speaker should mention himself last.*

1. Frank and —— are going to ride.
2. —— and —— have read the book.
3. Clara and —— will do your errand.
4. ——, ——, and —— are going together.
5. —— missed our train.
6. Edward and —— did the work.
7. Hear the children. —— are singing.
8. —— and —— went to Central Park.
9. Edith and —— were invited.

LESSON CXIX

OBJECTIVE FORMS OF PRONOUNS

Read these sentences, and tell which words are used as objects : —

1. I saw Henry.
2. I saw *him.*
3. He went with the boys.
4. He went with *them.*
5. She gave the flowers to Elizabeth and *me.*
6. She gave the flowers to *her* and *me.*
7. She gave the flowers to *us.*

Name the pronouns, and tell for what word each is used. Which pronouns are the objects of verbs? Which are the objects of prepositions?

The words *me, him, her, us,* and *them* take the place of nouns used as objects.

The form of a pronoun used as the object of a verb or of a preposition is the *objective form.*

EXERCISE

Copy the following sentences, and fill the blanks with the objective forms, me, him, her, us, or them : —

1. Grace called, and Dorothy went home with ——.
2. That book was given to —— and ——.
3. Our friends did not wait for ——.
4. The hunters took their guns with ——.
5. These things are common with ——.
6. His friends could not please ——.
7. The picture hung directly in front of ——.

LESSON CXX

POSSESSIVE FORMS OF PRONOUNS

Read the following sentences, and tell which words denote possession : —

1. I have lost *my* pencil.	7. Here is *his* hat.
2. This pencil is *mine*.	8. We lost *our* way.
3. This is *her* fan.	9. This carriage is *ours*.
4. This fan is *hers*.	10. Are these bees *yours?*
5. They met *their* friends.	11. Are these *your* bees?
6. These cabins are *theirs*.	12. The bird fell from *its* nest.

The form of a pronoun used to denote possession is the *possessive form*.

Which possessive forms above are used before the nouns they modify, and which forms are used after the noun?

EXERCISE 1

Copy these sentences, and draw a line under each word that denotes possession : —

1. Her eyes were blue.
2. These coats are theirs.
3. My horse stood near me.
4. We lost our way in the wood.
5. Are these slippers yours?
6. The drooping flower raised its head.
7. The black hat is mine.
8. They pitched their tents near our dwelling.
9. Are these trunks yours?
10. Two of them are ours.

Write sentences containing the following words. Never use the apostrophe with these possessive forms: —

my	yours	hers	their
mine	his	our	theirs
your	her	ours	its

LESSON CXXI

DICTATION EXERCISE

1. Most animals are provided with means by which to avoid or escape danger. Some creatures are of such a color that they are not readily seen as long as they remain motionless. Thus the giraffe may easily be overlooked as he stands amidst the leafless stems of dead trees.

2. Those creatures whose bulk or color is such as to render them easily visible are usually provided with keen sight and scent, and also with great speed. Thus the ostrich from its contrast to the plains on which it feeds can readily be seen at a distance. The bird is therefore provided with a keenness of vision and a speed unrivalled by any other creature.

3. Beasts of prey are usually so tinted that they can hardly be distinguished from the ground or the foliage amidst which they prowl. A lion in the long dry grass of an African plain or a tiger amidst dark brown or black weeds in an Indian jungle is almost invisible. Such animals by means of their padded feet can move about in the most silent manner. Thus guarded against detection by eyes or ears they easily procure their prey.

LESSON CXXII

ORAL COMPOSITION

EXERCISE 1

Read the following story : —

ARACHNE[1]

Arachne lived on the shores of the Mediterranean, and was famous for her skill in spinning and weaving and in embroidery.

A little shellfish was found in the sea near her home, from which men obtained a very beautiful dye called Tyrian purple. Arachne's father used to dye his wool in this rich purple color. Then Arachne spun this purple wool, and drew out the threads so long and so fine that they looked as filmy as the mists that hang over the sea.

Now, the goddess Athene had first taught the children of men how to spin the wool from the sheep, and then how to weave it into cloth; she had also taught them all the arts of the needle. So, when people saw how skilful Arachne was in these things, they said she must have been taught by Athene, meaning that she was inspired in her work by Athene.

But Arachne insisted that she owed all her skill to herself alone. She even went so far as to say that she should like to weave in competition with the goddess Athene, to see which could weave the better.

Then a bent old woman came to her, and tried to per-

---

[1] Arachne (*a-rak'-nē*).

suade her to be thankful to Athene for her great skill; but Arachne said some very boastful things, and was very disrespectful. Then the bent old woman threw off her cloak, and all at once grew tall and beautiful, and Arachne saw that it was the goddess . Athene herself. Still Arachne would not give the goddess the honor, but was willing to weave with her, as she had said.

Then Athene and Arachne each wove a wonderful tapestry. Athene's was covered with beautiful pictures; but Arachne's, although very skilful, represented all sorts of wicked things, for Arachne felt very spiteful when she was weaving.

When the tapestries were finished, and Athene saw what Arachne had done, she sprinkled her with the juice of a strange, poisonous plant, and changed her into a spider.

To this day the children of Arachne spin webs of wondrous fineness, but beware of their bite, for they are ever ready to show their venom.

EXERCISE 2

Tell in your own words the story of "Arachne."

LESSON CXXIII

WORDS AFTER *IS* AND *WAS*

Use the words *it is* with *I, he, she, we,* or *they,* in answering the following questions : —

1. Who is knocking at my door?
2. Is that Harold in the boat?

3. Is that your sister?

4. Is it you and Walter that wish to go?

5. Is it your cousins who are singing?

Example. — *Question.*   Who is knocking at my door?

            Answer.   It is I.

EXERCISE 1

Copy the following questions, and write an answer to each question, using in your answer, the words **it was** *with* **I, he, she, we,** *or* **they :** —

1. Was it your father and mother that entered the house?
2. Was it the postman that rang the bell?
3. Was it you that left the book?
4. Was it Helen that drew this picture?
5. Was it you and Florence that called to see me?

EXERCISE 2

Change these statements to questions.   Write the questions : —

It is I	It was I
It is he	It was he
It is she	It was she
It is we	It was we
It is they	It was they
It is we that must go	It was he or she
It is he or they	It was he that spoke

EXERCISE 8

Copy the following sentences, and fill the blanks with **I,** *we, he, she, or they :* —

1. Who raised the window?   It was ——.
2. Who is there?   It is ——.
3. Was that your brother?   It was ——.
4. It is —— who are reciting.
5. It was —— that brought the flowers.
6. Was it the boys?   It was ——.
7. Was it the Mayor in the first carriage?   It was ——.
8. Was it ——?   It is ——.
9. Is it ——?   It was ——.
10. It was —— that replied.
11. It was either —— or ——.
12. If —— were ——, —— would go.

LESSON CXXIV

COMPOSITION

THE RAINBOW

Write a description of " The Rainbow."

1. Tell what kind of weather brings the rainbow and when you saw one.

2. Tell what time of day you saw it, where the sun was, and where you looked for the rainbow.

3. Describe the rainbow — tell its form, name its colors, and tell in what order they appear.

4. Tell any story that you have heard about the rainbow.

LESSON CXXV

WORDS THAT CONNECT

1. The passengers took their seats, and the train started.

2. He owns the house, but he does not live in it.

3. The basket contained apples and oranges.

4. The pupils march and sing.

How many statements are made in the first sentence? Read each statement. What word joins the two statements?

How many sentences can you form from the second sentence? Read each. What word joins the two sentences?

What does *and* connect in the third sentence? In the fourth sentence?

A word that connects sentences or similar parts of the same sentence is a *conjunction*.

EXERCISE 1

Find the conjunctions in these sentences, and tell what they connect: —

1. The door opened, and the boy came in.

2. Walking and rowing expand the chest and strengthen the muscles.

3. The kettle was singing, and the clock was ticking.

4. Shall we walk or ride?

5. The notes of the wren are sharp and shrill.

6. He did not like the man's appearance, so he dismissed him.

7. We called at the house, but we did not see our friends.

8. The boy seemed pleased, yet he would not speak.

Copy the following sentences, and underline the conjunctions: —

1. Now stir the fire, and close the shutters **fast.**
2. Is this a time to be cloudy and sad?
3. Days brightly came and calmly went.
4. She trimmed the lamp and made it **bright,**
   And left it swinging to and fro.
5. Our band is few, but true and tried.
6. Sink or swim, live or die, survive or **perish, I give** my hand and my heart to this vote.
7. They came, but they did not **stay.**
8. Her voice was low and sweet.
9. Will you walk or ride?
10. Speak clearly if you would be understood.

Copy the following lines, and commit them to memory: —

> Farewell, farewell! but this I tell
>   To thee, thou Wedding-Guest!
> He prayeth well who loveth well
>   Both man and bird and beast.
>
> He prayeth best who loveth best
>   All things both great and small;
> For the dear God who loveth us,
>   He made and loveth all.
>   —SAMUEL TAYLOR COLERIDGE.

LESSON CXXVI

A PICTURE LESSON

Corot

THE COTTAGE

EXERCISE 1

Where does this cottage stand? Describe it. What do you see around the cottage? What life do you notice about the place? What time of the year is it? How do you know? Who do you think lives in this cottage?

EXERCISE 2

Write a story suggested by this picture.

LESSON CXXVII

INTERJECTIONS

1. Hark! I hear quails.
2. Hush! they will hear us.

Read the assertion in each sentence.

Which word in the first example forms no part of the assertion? What is the use of the word *hark*?

Which word in the second example forms no part of the assertion? Why is it used?

Words like *hark* and *hush* are added to sentences to indicate sudden or intense feeling. Such words are called **interjections.**

Sometimes an interjection is used with other words in an exclamatory phrase; as, —

O noble judge! O excellent young man!

The interjection *O* should be written as a capital letter.

An exclamatory word, phrase, or sentence should be followed by the exclamation point.

EXERCISE

Copy the following sentences, and notice where the exclamation point is placed: —

1. Hark! was it the wind that rustled the leaves?
2. Alas! I can go no farther.
3. Ah! is that the cause of his complaint?
4. Away! we must not linger.
5. "Hello! come back," called the boy.
6. A horse! a horse! my kingdom for a horse!
7. Our country calls; away! away!
8. Hist! I hear footsteps.

LESSON CXXVIII

DICTATION EXERCISE

1. Alas! what will become of the poor sailors?
2. Ho! ho! the breakers roared.
3. Ah! there they are.
4. Help! help! the boat is sinking.
5. Thou hast all seasons for thine own, O Death!
6. Hark! 'tis the twanging horn o'er yonder bridge.
7. O mighty Cæsar! dost thou lie so low?
8. Lo! how all things fade and perish!

LESSON CXXIX

PARTS OF SPEECH

SUMMARY OF FACTS ABOUT THE USES OF WORDS

A word used as a name is a *noun ;* as, *Arthur* rode the *horse.* *Stars* twinkle.

A word used for a noun is a *pronoun ;* as, *I* walked. *You* came. *They* went home.

A word used to modify the meaning of a noun or pronoun is an *adjective ;* as, *Tall* oaks from *little* acorns grow. We are *seven.* Look at *this* picture.

A word that asserts is a *verb ;* as, The sun *shines.* Birds *build* nests. Ice *is* cold.

A word that modifies the meaning of a verb, an adjective, or another adverb is an *adverb ;* as, The rain falls *gently.* The room is *too* small. He walked *very* slowly.

A word used with a noun or pronoun to show its relation to some other word in the sentence is a *preposition;* as, They sailed *down* the harbor.   Speak *to* him.

A word that connects sentences or similar parts of the same sentence is a *conjunction;* as, The bell rang, *and* the boat started. The sun shines, *but* the air is cold.   The notes of the wren are sharp *and* shrill.

A word used to indicate sudden or intense feeling is an *interjection;* as, *Alas!* our friends had gone.

Words are thus divided into eight different classes according to their uses in the sentence.   These different classes of words are called **parts of speech.**

EXERCISE

Write sentences containing the following: —

1. A noun.
2. A pronoun.
3. An adjective.
4. A verb.
5. An adverb.
6. A preposition.
7. A conjunction.
8. An interjection.

In each one of your sentences underline the part of speech illustrated.

PART THIRD

---•⚬✦⚬•---

LESSON CXXX

USES OF SENTENCES

1. The box was filled with old coins.
2. Make a good use of your time.
3. What did you see?
4. How refreshing the rain is!

State the use of each sentence above — tell what it does.

A sentence that states or declares something is a *declarative sentence;* as, —

The car was loaded with wheat.

A sentence that expresses a command or an entreaty is an *imperative sentence;* as, —

Turn to the right.
Keep thy tongue from evil.

A sentence that asks a question is an *interrogative sentence;* as, —

Where shall we go?

A sentence that expresses sudden or strong feeling is an *exclamatory sentence;* as, —

> How cold this water is!
> What a brave deed that was!

A complete sentence, not interrogative or exclamatory, should be followed by a period.

An interrogative sentence should be followed by the interrogation point.

An exclamatory sentence should be followed by the exclamation point.

EXERCISE 1

In each of the following examples, tell whether the sentence is declarative, imperative, interrogative, or exclamatory: —

1. These flowers grow by the roadside.
2. The message will be delivered this afternoon.
3. Can you see the lighthouse?
4. Love your enemies.
5. What a long day it has been!
6. I saw a flock of beach birds.
7. Lead us not into temptation.
8. What a strong arm the blacksmith has!

EXERCISE 2

Write declarative sentences telling how the animals named below move about from one point to another: —

cows	fishes	snakes	hares
birds	turtles	toads	horses

EXERCISE 3

Write imperative sentences that might be addressed to —

a child	a dressmaker	a bookseller
a dog	a florist	a class of pupils
a coachman	a grocer	a company of soldiers

EXERCISE 4

Write interrogative sentences about —

the stars	clouds	rivers	valleys
the wind	lakes	icebergs	mountains

EXERCISE 5

Write an exclamatory sentence about —

a sunset	a warm day	a cricket
a rainbow	a snow-storm	a grasshopper

LESSON CXXXI

SELECTION TO BE MEMORIZED

Read the following poem, and commit it to memory: —

JUNE

(From "The Vision of Sir Launfal")

And what is so rare as a day in June?
  Then, if ever, come perfect days;
Then Heaven tries earth if it be in tune,
  And over it softly her warm ear lays;
Whether we look, or whether we listen,
We hear life murmur, or see it glisten;
Every clod feels a stir of might,

An instinct within it that reaches and towers,
And, groping blindly above it for light,
  Climbs to a soul in grass and flowers;
The flush of life may well be seen
  Thrilling back over hills and valleys;
The cowslip startles in meadows green,
  The buttercup catches the sun in its chalice,
And there's never a leaf nor a blade too mean
  To be some happy creature's palace;
The little bird sits at his door in the sun,
  Atilt like a blossom among the leaves,
And lets his illumined being o'errun
  With the deluge of summer it receives;
His mate feels the eggs beneath her wings,
And the heart in her dumb breast flutters and sings;
He sings to the wide world, and she to her nest, —
In the nice ear of Nature which song is the best?
                       — JAMES RUSSELL LOWELL.

LESSON CXXXII

SUBJECT AND PREDICATE

1. Ice melts.
2. Wood burns.
3. Smoke rises.

Tell what each sentence is about, and what is said about the thing named.

Every sentence consists of two parts. One part names that about which something is said; the other part tells what is said or asserted about the thing named.

The part of a sentence that names that about which something is asserted is the *subject*.

The part of a sentence that tells what is asserted about the person or thing named by the subject is the *predicate*.

The subject may be expressed by a single word, or by two or more words ; as, *Leaves* fall. *Dead leaves* fall. *The dead leaves fall.*

The predicate may also be expressed by a single word, or by two or more words ; as, Bells *ring*. Bells *are ringing*. Bells *are ringing merrily.*

EXERCISE 1

Copy the following sentences, filling the blanks with suitable subjects : —

1. —— bark.	4. —— cackle.	7. —— hoot.
2. —— mew.	5. —— crow.	8. —— caw.
3. —— bleat.	6. —— squeal.	9. —— coo.

EXERCISE 2

Copy the following sentences, filling the blanks with suitable predicates : —

1. Horses ——.	4. Lions ——.	7. Frogs ——.
2. Cows ——.	5. Wolves ——.	8. Bees ——.
3. Donkeys ——.	6. Foxes ——.	9. Crickets ——.

EXERCISE 3

Copy the following sentences, and in each example draw one line under the subject and two lines under the predicate : —

1. Aladdin had a wonderful lamp.
2. Two sailors landed on an island.

3. The island was covered with trees.
4. A large ship entered the harbor.
5. The cherry tree has white blossoms.
6. The merry party reached the top of the hill.
7. White clouds were sailing in the sky.
8. Birds were singing in the trees.
9. We saw bright-colored butterflies.
10. Spring days are delightful.

LESSON CXXXIII

TRANSPOSED ORDER

1. The masts came down.
2. Down came the masts.
3. The night grew darker.
4. Darker grew the night.

Notice the order of the subject and the predicate in the examples above. In which of these sentences is the subject placed first? In which is the predicate placed first?

The subject of a declarative sentence is usually placed before the predicate. This order of parts is called the **usual order**. But sometimes, especially in poetry, the subject is placed after the predicate. This order is called the **transposed order**.

EXERCISE 1

Point out the subject and the predicate in each of the following sentences, and tell which sentences are in the transposed order: —

1. The trees were in full leaf.
2. Away flew the bird.
3. A little cottage stood near the bay.
4. She lifted the box carefully.
5. On a table lies his silver-hilted sword.
6. In a corner of the room stands his gold-headed cane.
7. Wide open stood the gates.
8. Blessed are the peacemakers.

EXERCISE 2

Re-write these sentences, arranging them in the usual order with the subject before the predicate : —

1. Here stood the famous tree.
2. Down plunged the diver.
3. Up came the treasure in abundance.
4. At the head of the table sat the Governor.
5. Not far from the gateway was the bridge.
6. Near this spot were the large warehouses.
7. Here might be seen some of the prosperous merchants.
8. Silently fell the snow.

LESSON CXXXIV

IMPERATIVE SENTENCES

The subject of an imperative sentence is *thou*, *ye*, or *you*. It is seldom expressed; thus, —

Look at this picture.

EXERCISE

Copy the following sentences, supplying the subjects that are understood and enclosing them in brackets : —

1. Open the gate quickly.
2. Water the flowers in the garden.
3. Learn to use your eyes.
4. Look at this spider's web.
5. Never lose a chance of saying a kind word.
6. Hear this account of the accident.
7. Set the tree firmly.
8. Gather the ripe fruit.

Example. — [You] open the gate quickly.

LESSON CXXXV

STUDY OF POEM

ABOU BEN ADHEM

Abou Ben Adhem (may his tribe increase!)
Awoke one night from a deep dream of peace,
And saw, within the moonlight in his room,
Making it rich, and like a lily in bloom,
An Angel writing in a book of gold : —
Exceeding peace had made Ben Adhem bold,
And to the Presence in the room he said,
"What writest thou?" — The Vision raised its head,
And with a look made of all sweet accord
Answered, "The names of those who love the Lord."
"And is mine one?" said Abou. "Nay, not so,"

Replied the Angel. Abou spoke more low,
But cheerily still, and said, "I pray tnee, then,
Write me as one that loves his fellow men."

The Angel wrote and vanished. The next night
It came again with a great wakening light,
And showed the names whom love of God had blessed,
And, lo! Ben Adhem's name led all the rest.

— LEIGH HUNT.

EXERCISE 1

Tell in your own words the story of "Abou Ben Adhem."

EXERCISE 2

Copy this poem, and commit it to memory.

LESSON CXXXVI

INTERROGATIVE SENTENCES

1. The apples are ripe.
2. Are the apples ripe?

Read these sentences and tell what kind of sentence each example is.

Name the subject and the predicate in the declarative sentence.

What is the subject in the interrogative sentence? What is the predicate? Where is the subject placed?

The subject of an interrogative sentence is usually placed after the predicate, or after the first word of the predicate; as, —

Where are *the flowers?* Has *the book* been found?

EXERCISE

Copy the following sentences, and in each example draw one line under the subject and two lines under the predicate : —

1. Can you row a boat?
2. How did you cross the river?
3. What do you see?
4. How much does this pitcher hold?
5. Has this fountain a name?
6. How many birds are in the nest?
7. Can the young birds fly?
8. Upon what does the swallow feed?
9. Why does the swallow fly about so much?
10. What is a bird of passage?   •

LESSON CXXXVII

EXCLAMATORY SENTENCES

EXERCISE

Copy the following sentences, and point out the subject and the predicate in each example : —

1. What a grand old tree this is!
2. How welcome is the shade!
3. How stately the old house looks!
4. What a wonderful place this is!
5. How long and green the grass is!
6. How the water sparkles!
7. How beautiful is the rain!
8. How excellent is thy loving kindness!

LESSON CXXXVIII

DICTATION EXERCISE

(From " The Planting of the Apple Tree ")

What plant we in this apple tree?
Buds, which the breath of summer days
Shall lengthen into leafy sprays;
Boughs, where the thrush, with crimson breast,
Shall haunt and sing and hide her nest ;
We plant, upon the sunny lea,
A shadow for the noontide hour,
A shelter from the summer shower,
When we plant the apple tree.

— WILLIAM CULLEN BRYANT.

LESSON CXXXIX

PHRASES

1. She wore a *gold* ring.
2. She wore a ring *of gold*.
3. The tree stood *here*.
4. The tree stood *in this place*.

What part of speech is the word *gold* in the first sentence? In the second sentence, find a combination of words used like an adjective.

What part of speech is the word *here* in the third sentence?

In the fourth sentence, find a combination of words used like an adverb.

A combination of words performing a distinct office in a sentence, but having neither subject nor predicate, is a *phrase*.

A phrase that performs the office of an adjective is an *adjective phrase*; as, —

The life of man is brief.

A phrase that performs the office of an adverb is an *adverbial phrase*; as, —

The clock ticked in the corner.

EXERCISE 1

Copy the following sentences, and draw lines under the phrases : —

1. The little stream ran under a wooden bridge.
2. The children are playing by the lake.
3. In the corner was a brass bedstead.
4. The roof of the church is steep.
5. Many of our birds use hair in their nests.
6. I hear the spring note of the chickadee.
7. The ice on the pond is softened.
8. What is the earliest sign of spring?
9. The fishes are going up the brooks.
10. The buds of the shad-blossom look green.

EXERCISE 2

Write five sentences containing adjective phrases.

EXERCISE 3

Write five sentences containing adverbial phrases.

LESSON CXL

ADJECTIVE PHRASES

EXERCISE 1

Re-write the following sentences, substituting equivalent phrases for the italicized adjectives: —

1. It was a *beautiful* rose.
2. A *wooden* bridge spanned the river.
3. He lost a *valuable* ring.
4. The leader was a *courageous* man.
5. The child wore a *flannel* suit.
6. *American* soldiers are brave.
7. Wild cattle roam over *vast* fields.
8. *Brass* candlesticks were on the mantel.

Example. — It was a *beautiful* rose.

It was a rose *of great beauty*.

EXERCISE 2

Point out the adjective phrases in the following examples, and tell what each phrase modifies: —

1. The leaves of the lilac are heart-shaped.
2. The course of the ship was changed.
3. A bouquet of wild flowers stood on the table.
4. Have you seen the new house on the corner?
5. The branches of the hemlock are very numerous.
6. The bark of the hemlock is used in tanning.
7. Listen to the murmur of the brook.
8. There are vast mines of gold in this island.
9. Here we found a spring of fresh water.

LESSON CXLI

ADVERBIAL PHRASES

EXERCISE 1

Re-write the following sentences, substituting equivalent phrases for the italicized adverbs: —

1. We sat *here* for a long time.
2. He removed the soil *carefully*.
3. The clouds are moving *rapidly*.
4. What have you *there?*
5. The work will be done *soon*.
6. I will *now* listen to your story.
7. The gardener answered our questions *cheerfully*.
8. Do not read the letter *now*.
9. Was the coat made *properly?*
10. He ran into the house *excitedly*.

Example. — We sat *here* for a long time.

We sat *in this place* for a long time.

EXERCISE 2

Point out the adverbial phrases in the following sentences, and tell what each phrase modifies: —

1. A young bird sat on the garden wall.
2. The boat sailed up the river.
3. We were received with open arms.
4. Their ship was wrecked on this island.
5. These bulbs are left in the ground all summer.
6. In the morning, we proceeded on our journey.
7. Woodpeckers drum on dry limbs.

8. The raindrops glistened on the trees.
9. Jacob went down into Egypt.
10. Crossbills were feeding in the pines.

LESSON CXLII

STUDY OF SELECTION

THE GLADNESS OF NATURE

I

Is this a time to be cloudy and sad,
  When our mother Nature laughs around;
When even the deep blue heavens look glad,
  And gladness breathes from the blossoming ground?

II

There are notes of joy from the hang-bird and wren,
  And the gossip of swallows through all the sky;
The ground-squirrel gayly chirps by his den,
  And the wilding bee hums merrily by.

III

The clouds are at play in the azure space,
  And their shadows at play on the bright green vale,
And here they stretch to the frolic chase,
  And there they roll on the easy gale.

IV

There's a dance of leaves in that aspen bower,
  There's a titter of winds in that beechen tree,
There's a smile on the fruit, and a smile on the flower,
  And a laugh from the brook that runs to the sea.

V

And look at the broad-faced sun, how he smiles
On the dewy earth that smiles in his ray,
On the leaping waters and gay young isles;
Ay, look, and he'll smile thy gloom away.

— WILLIAM CULLEN BRYANT.

Read the first stanza. What does this stanza do? Read the first line of the question. How many reasons are given in this stanza for not being *cloudy* and *sad?* State each. What is meant by *our mother Nature?* Why is she said to be laughing?

Read the second stanza. What does the first line tell? What is a hang-bird? What kind of nest does it build? What is the second line about? What are the swallows said to be doing? What does the squirrel do? How does he chirp? Where does he chirp? What is the fourth line about? What is the meaning of *wilding?*

Read the third stanza. What is the first line about? Name the phrases in this line and tell the use of each. What is meant by the *azure space?* What does *their* refer to in the second line? What were the shadows doing? Does the third line refer to the shadows or to the clouds? What does the fourth line refer to?

Read the fourth stanza. In this stanza, how many different things are said to express pleasure? Name the different things and tell what actions are ascribed to them.

Read the last stanza. At what is the reader directed to look? What is the sun said to be doing? Why is the reader told to look at the sun?

EXERCISE

Copy the poem about "The Gladness of Nature" and commit it to memory.

LESSON CXLIII

LETTER-WRITING

EXERCISE

You are visiting a friend.

Write a letter to some member of your family who is at home, telling how you are spending your time, and describing a place of interest that you have visited.

LESSON CXLIV

CLAUSES

1. You will change your plans if you are wise.
2. The car stopped when the bell rang.

How many assertions are made in each of the sentences above ? Give the subject and the predicate in each assertion.

A combination of words performing a distinct office in a sentence, and having a subject and a predicate, is a *clause*.

A clause that expresses the leading or principal thought of a sentence is an *independent* or *principal clause;* as, —

If our cause is just, *we shall succeed.*

A clause that depends upon some other part of the sentence for its full meaning is a *dependent* or *subordinate clause;* as, —

If our cause is just, we shall succeed.

EXERCISE

Copy the following sentences, and draw lines under the dependent clauses :—

1. The night cometh, when no man can work.

2. Hear me, for I will speak.

3. If the ground is too wet, the plants will not grow.

4. This tree will flourish, for it has struck its roots deep.

5. The people murmured as their suffering increased.

6. As we approached the house, we heard the sound of music.

7. They will return when the matter is decided.

8. We came to a point where four paths met.

LESSON CXLV

RELATIVE PRONOUNS

1. The general, *who is an excellent horseman*, kept his seat.

2. They entered this path, *which is steep*.

3. He *that is giddy* thinks the world turns round.

In each of the examples above, point out the principal clause and the dependent clause.

Find in each dependent clause a word that refers to a preceding noun or pronoun, and tell how the dependent clause is joined to the principal clause.

A pronoun that refers or relates to a noun or another pronoun and joins to it a dependent clause is a *relative pronoun*.

The noun or pronoun to which a relative pronoun refers or relates is called its **antecedent**, because the antecedent usually precedes the pronoun ; as, —

The *boy who* delivered the message is not here.

They that touch pitch will be defiled.

Copy the following sentences, and underline the relative pronouns and their antecedents :—

1. He who is not master of himself cannot control others.

2. The weather, which had been fine, now changed.

3. The children, who had been waiting outside the door, entered the room joyfully.

4. These fields, which were forty feet square, resembled so many beds of flowers.

5. A sharp tongue is the only instrument that grows keener with constant use.

6. The paths that lead to the castle are carefully guarded.

7. The cell of the bee is built at that angle which gives the most strength with the least wax.

8. Birds are not the only animals that migrate.

9. The journeys which the salmon make are as regular and remarkable as those of birds.

10. Sometimes from lack of food insects migrate. This has been shown by the swarms of grasshoppers which have swept through some of our Western States.

LESSON CXLVI

COMPOSITION

OUR SONG BIRDS

Write about "Our Song Birds."

1. Tell what the most common song birds are in your locality.

2. Give, as fully as you can, facts relating to their food supply, and show their great value to man.

3. Mention some of the natural enemies of birds, such as cats, owls, snakes, etc.

4. Tell how birds have been destroyed through the action of egg-collectors and sportsmen.

5. Show what the effect of using birds for millinery purposes has been, and tell what you know about the societies that have been formed to prevent their destruction.

LESSON CXLVII

ADJECTIVE CLAUSES

1. Is this the book that was lost?

2. The chair was made of oak, which had grown dark with age.

Read the dependent clause in the first sentence. What does it modify?

Read the second sentence. Which is the explanatory clause in this example? What does it modify?

A clause that performs the office of an adjective is an *adjective clause*.

EXERCISE

Copy the following sentences, and underline the adjective clauses and the words which they modify: —

1. Did you ever hear of the golden apples that grew in the garden of the Hesperides?

2. Many people doubted whether there could be real trees that bore apples of solid gold upon their branches.

3. Adventurous young men, who desired to do a braver

thing than any of their fellows, set out in quest of this fruit.

4. None of them brought back the apples that grew on the golden apple tree.

5. It is said that the tree was guarded by a terrible dragon, which had a hundred heads. Fifty of these heads were always on the watch, while the other fifty slept.

LESSON CXLVIII

SELECTIONS TO BE MEMORIZED

Read the following poems, and commit them to memory: —

I

A BOY'S SONG

Where the pools are bright and deep,
Where the gray trout lies asleep,
Up the river and o'er the lea,
That's the way for Billy and me.

Where the blackbird sings the latest,
Where the hawthorn blooms the sweetest,
Where the nestlings chirp and flee,
That's the way for Billy and me.

Where the mowers mow the cleanest,
Where the hay lies thick and greenest,
There to trace the homeward bee,
That's the way for Billy and me.

Where the hazel bank is steepest,
Where the shadow falls the deepest,
Where the clustering nuts fall free,
That's the way for Billy and me.

                 —JAMES HOGG.

II

THE THROSTLE

"Summer is coming, summer is coming.
I know it, I know it, I know it.
Light again, leaf again, life again, love again,"
Yes, my wild little Poet.

Sing the new year in under the blue.
Last year you sang it as gladly.
"New, new, new, new"! Is it then so new
That you should carol so madly?

"Love again, song again, nest again, young again,
Never a prophet so crazy!
And hardly a daisy as yet, little friend,
See, there is hardly a daisy.

"Here again, here, here, here, happy year!"
O warble unchidden, unbidden.
Summer is coming, is coming, my dear,
And all the winters are hidden.

                 —ALFRED TENNYSON.

LESSON CXLIX

ADVERBIAL CLAUSES

1. Leave the boat where it can be found.
2. When the apples are ripe, they will fall.

In the first example, point out the principal clause and the dependent clause. What does the dependent clause tell?

Read the principal clause in the second example. Read the dependent clause. What does the dependent clause modify?

A clause that performs the office of an adverb is an *adverbial clause*.

EXERCISE

Point out the adverbial clauses in the following examples, and tell what each clause modifies: —

1. When the bees carry in their first pollen, one would think spring had come.
2. They soon came to a beach, where the great waves were beating upon the hard sand.
3. Moses was a hundred and twenty years old when he died.
4. The ball fell where you are standing.
5. An honest man speaks as he thinks.
6. This tree must be planted where the soil is moist.
7. We started on our journey before the sun rose.
8. The stable was locked after the horse was stolen.
9. Strike while the iron is hot.
10. Make hay while the sun shines.

LESSON CL

LETTER-WRITING

EXERCISE

Write a letter to your mother, who has been away from home for two weeks.

Tell about the health of the family, and give any items of home or neighborhood news that she would like to know.

LESSON CLI

ORAL COMPOSITION

EXERCISE 1

Read the following story : —

BALDER

Balder, the beautiful, Balder, the bright, shining god, dreamed one night that he was wandering in the silent lower world, the world of the dead. Three nights he dreamed this dream. Then he told his father Odin, and his mother Frigga, and their hearts were filled with fear.

Then Frigga, mounted on a swift black horse, rode to the end of the world. Nine days and nine nights she rode, and she asked everything she met to promise to do no harm to Balder. Fire and water, stones and trees, metals, beasts, birds, and all creeping things gave the promise; for all things loved Balder. But the mistletoe she did not ask, because it was so small and weak.

Then the gods made a sport of throwing sticks and stones at Balder, to see how they fell from him without hurting him. They even threw their spears and other war-like weapons at him, but not one of the gods would willingly have hurt him.

Loki, who was always spiteful and selfish, came by one day, when this sport was going on. He was jealous of Balder, because none of these things would hurt him, and he immediately began to contrive a wicked plan. Craftily disguising himself as an old woman with things to sell, he visited Frigga's house, and found out that the mistletoe had given no promise not to hurt Balder. Then he brought a twig of mistletoe, and gave it to the blind god, Höder, inviting him to join in the sport, by throwing something at Balder.

So, Höder, not knowing what he was doing, threw the mistletoe, and instantly Balder fell down dead.

Then all the gods wept; the earth grew dark and cold, all the little singing birds flew away, and the flowers dropped their leaves.

Then Frigga sent a messenger to Hela's dark kingdom, to ask that Balder might return to earth. Hela said that if all living things and all things without life would weep for Balder, he might return. Loki, alone, would not weep.

When Odin, the father of the gods, saw that Loki would not weep for Balder, his anger was terrible, and Loki was afraid and hid himself under a mountain.

When Loki, who is the cause of all the selfishness and wrong-doing in the world, is conquered, Balder will come again.

EXERCISE 2

Tell in your own words the story of " Balder."

LESSON CLII

POSITION OF MODIFIERS

1. The book had a bright red cover.
2. Only two persons entered the room.
3. I have not read the letter.

Read the sentences. What kind of *red cover* did the book have? Notice that the word *bright* modifies the expression *red cover*.

How many persons entered the room? What word modifies *two*? Where is it placed?

What does *not* modify in the third example? Where is it placed?

Place each modifier as near as possible to the word that it modifies.

EXERCISE

Re-write the following sentences, inserting in each example the word from the parenthesis. Be careful to place each word so that it will express the meaning intended: —

1. They were here three days. (only)
2. The heron's bill was six inches long. (nearly)
3. He gave the boy two silver dollars. (bright)
4. There was a spring of water in the wood. (cool)
5. Did you visit the Ladies' Home? (Old)
6. Do you keep ladies' silk gloves? (black)
7. I paddled along the south shore. (near)
8. There were two letters in the box. (only)
9. Have you seen our boys' suits? (flannel)

10. I have read the book. (not)

11. Packs of dogs came rushing forth. (savage)

12. Herds of bay horses neighed shrilly as we rode past them. (dark)

LESSON CLIII

COMPOSITION

YELLOWSTONE PARK

Write a description of "Yellowstone Park."

1. Tell where Yellowstone Park is, give its area, and tell something of its surface.

2. Describe some of its great natural curiosities.

3. Tell what you know about the wild animals that live in the Park, and what the United States government has done for their care and protection.

LESSON CLIV

PHRASE MODIFIERS

EXERCISE

Re-write the following sentences, inserting in the proper places the phrases from the parentheses: —

1. Our party hired a little steamer called the Owl. (for one day)

2. Passengers are requested to purchase tickets. (before entering the cars, at the company's office)

3. I started out for a trip up the Hudson River. (in a sailboat)

4. He supported his family by cutting wood. (in a neighboring forest)

5. The flag was shot away. (at the masthead)

6. The tree was for shelter. (above them)

7. He was sentenced to jail for disorderly conduct. (for ten days)

8. A young man desires a room fronting the south. (of studious habits)

9. In this room is a portrait of the General. (over the mantel-piece)

10. A basket stood on the sideboard. (of fruit)

LESSON CLV

CLAUSE MODIFIERS

EXERCISE

Re-write the following sentences, inserting in the proper places the clauses from the parentheses: —

1. The flowers are those in the eastern part of the Park. (which spring up first)

2. The Greeks were very fond of all sports. (which could make the body strong)

3. He whispered to the rifleman to take his rifle. (who sat kneeling in the bow of the boat)

4. The boat now lay unused under the gangway. (which had taken the party ashore)

5. A bird avoids the snare. (that is cautious)

6. This was the only voyage in all my adventures. (which was successful)

7. He conquers his greatest enemy. (who masters his passions)

8. The grapes were raised in a hothouse. (which we had for breakfast)

9. Have you returned the book to the library? (which you borrowed)

10. He leans on a broken reed. (that leans on his own strength)

LESSON CLVI

LETTER-WRITING

EXERCISE

Your uncle sent you a book for a birthday present.

Write a letter to your uncle, thanking him for the gift, and telling him why you specially like the book.

LESSON CLVII

FORMS OF SENTENCES

1. The wind blew.
2. When the wind changed, the air grew cooler.
3. The wind blew, and the rain fell.

How many thoughts are expressed in the first example above?

How many thoughts are expressed in the second example? Tell which is the principal clause, and which the subordinate clause in this sentence.

How many sentences can you form from the third example? Read the independent parts or members of the third sentence.

A sentence that expresses one thought is a *simple sentence*; as, —

> The river has a steep bank.
> Fasten the boat to the wharf.
> Can you row a boat?
> How clear the water is!

A sentence consisting of one principal clause and one or more subordinate clauses is a *complex sentence*; as, —

If you try, you will succeed.

This man, who has charge of the building, will show you the room.

A sentence made up of two or more independent members is a *compound sentence*; as, —

Be just, and fear not.

He passed the tree in safety, but new perils lay before him.

EXERCISE

Point out the simple, the complex, and the compound sentences in the following examples, and tell of what clauses the complex and the compound sentences are composed: —

1. She stepped quickly across the floor.
2. If you cannot sleep, you can rest.
3. If you would find the most wretched man or woman in your neighborhood, look for the one who has nothing to do.
4. They were startled by the tramp of horses' hoofs.
5. He had won great fame among the children, as the narrator of wonderful stories.

6. Sponges are the skeletons of small marine animals.

7. He entered the room softly, but she heard his step.

8. A soft answer turneth away wrath, but grievous words stir up anger.

9. The sun was setting as they entered the village.

10. If you will listen, I will tell you the story.

11. My life's beset, my path is lost,
    The gale has chilled my limbs with frost.

12. When life is all sport, toil is the real play.

13. How slowly the boat moves!

14. Look at the shadows on the hillside.

15. The town had drifted behind us, and we were nearing the group of islands.

LESSON CLVIII

COMPOSITION

THE COCOA-NUT CRAB

Upon some of the coral islands in the Pacific Ocean you may find such strange and unique creatures as the famous cocoa-nut crab.

A great crab he is, who walks upon the tips of his toes a foot high above the ground. And because he has often nothing to eat but cocoa-nuts, or at least they are the best things he can find, cocoa-nuts he has learned to eat, and after a fashion which it would puzzle you to imitate. Some say that he climbs up the stems of the cocoa-nut trees, and pulls the fruit down for himself; but that, it seems, he does not usually do. What he does is this: when he finds a fallen cocoa-nut, he begins tearing away the thick husk and fibre with his strong claws; and he knows perfectly well which end to tear it from, namely, from the end where the three eye-holes are, which you call the monkey's face, out of one of which, you know, the young cocoa-nut tree would burst forth. And when he has got to the eye-holes, he hammers through one of them with the point of his heavy claw. So far, so good; but how is he to get the meat out? He cannot put his claw in. He has no proboscis like a butterfly to insert and suck with. He is as far off from his dinner as the fox was when the stork offered him a feast in a long-necked jar. What, then, do you think he does? He turns himself round, puts in a pair of his hind pincers, which are very slender, and with them scoops the meat out of the cocoa-nut, and so puts his dinner into his mouth with his hind feet.

And even the cocoa-nut husk he does not waste; for he lives in deep burrows which he makes, like a rabbit; and being a luxurious crab, and liking to sleep soft in spite of his hard shell, he lines them with a quantity of cocoa-nut fibre, picked out clear and fine, just as if he were going to make cocoa-nut matting of it.

And being also a clean crab, he goes down to the sea every night to have his bath and moisten his gills, and so lives happy all his days, and gets so fat in his old age that he carries about in his body nearly a quart of pure oil.

— CHARLES KINGSLEY, "MADAM HOW AND LADY WHY."

EXERCISE

Write in your own words an account of "The Cocoa-nut Crab." Follow this outline:—

1. Where the cocoa-nut crab is found.
2. His size and mode of walking.
3. His food and how he obtains it.
4. His burrows and his habits.

LESSON CLIX

SIMPLE SENTENCES

EXERCISE

In each of the following examples, (1) tell whether the sentence is declarative, imperative, interrogative, or exclamatory; and (2) give the subject and the predicate:—

1. Navigation on the Hudson stops about the last of November.
2. Have you ever seen an ice boat?
3. How swiftly it moves!
4. Look at the eagles.
5. The eagle seldom or never turns his back upon a storm.
6. The days are growing shorter.
7. He walked slowly up the hill.
8. Did you see the sun rise?
9. The boys entered the house quietly.
10. Do not forget the message.

11. Did the strangers lose their way?

12. What a graceful tree the elm is!

13. The wood of the oak is remarkable for its strength and toughness.

14. What a cold morning it is!

15. Listen to the cracking of the trees.

LESSON CLX

PUNCTUATION OF COMPOUND SENTENCES

In each of the following sentences, tell what mark is used to separate the members of the sentence : —

1. She turned the key, and the lid sprang back.

2. We visited the spot; but could find neither bush, bird, nor nest.

The members of a compound sentence, when short and closely connected, should be separated by the comma; as, —

The walls are high, and the shores are steep.

When the members of a compound sentence are subdivided by the comma, they are usually separated by the semicolon; as, —

He looked upon his people, and a tear was in his eye;
He looked upon the traitors, and his glance was stern
and high.

EXERCISE

Copy the following sentences, and place commas and semicolons wherever they are needed : —

1. The clock struck ten and the pupils rose from their seats.

2. The door opened and two children ran down the steps.

3. The forests have shed their leaves and the voices of the winter birds are heard.

4. Go to the ant thou sluggard consider her ways and be wise.

5. The swallows prepare for their annual migration and all things announce the speedy decline of summer.

6. We found the house but the doors were locked and the family was gone.

7. The table is large and it has two good drawers.

8. Few and short were the prayers we said
   And we spoke not a word of sorrow
   But we steadfastly gazed on the face that was dead
   And we bitterly thought of the morrow.

LESSON CLXI

COMPOSITION

A WESTERN RANCH

Write a description of "A Western Ranch."

1. Tell what a ranch is, and how it differs from a farm.

2. Describe the way in which the cattle and sheep are allowed to wander about from place to place, tell how the herdsmen keep track of them, and how a ranchman knows his own stock.

3. Describe the buildings and the manner of life on a ranch.

LESSON CLXII

SELECTIONS TO BE MEMORIZED

Copy the following selections, and commit them to memory:—

I

Breathes there the man with soul so dead,
Who never to himself hath said,
    "This is my own—my native land!"
Whose heart hath ne'er within him burned,
As home his footsteps he hath turned,
    From wandering on a foreign strand?
If such there breathe, go, mark him well!
For him no minstrel raptures swell;
High though his titles, proud his name,
Boundless his wealth as wish can claim,—
Despite those titles, power, and pelf,
The wretch, concentred all in self,
Living shall forfeit fair renown,
And, doubly dying, shall go down
To the vile dust from whence he sprung,
Unwept, unhonored, and unsung.

—SIR WALTER SCOTT.

II

Stand by the Flag! On land and ocean billow
    By it your fathers stood unmoved and true,
Living, defended; dying, from their pillow,
    With their last blessing, passed it on to you.

—JOHN NICHOLS WILDER.

LESSON CLXIII

COMPLEX SENTENCES

EXERCISE

In each of the following examples, combine the sentences into one complex sentence. Make such changes in the sentences as are necessary.

Example. — The storm did not cease, till the Atlantic was strewn with wrecks.

1. The storm did not cease. The Atlantic was strewn with wrecks.

2. The settlers made preparations to winter here. Cold weather was approaching.

3. The Emperor's horse was shod with gold. How did he come by golden shoes?

4. The Emperor's horse was a beautiful creature. His eyes were wise like a man's. His mane hung down his neck like a silk veil.

5. He had carried his master through the fire and smoke of battle. He had heard the bullets whistling around him. He had kicked. He had bitten. He had taken part in the fight.

6. He had saved the crown of red gold. He had saved the life of the Emperor. The life of the Emperor was of the greatest value.

7. For this reason, the Emperor's horse had golden shoes. He wore a golden shoe on each foot.

LESSON CLXIV

COMPOUND SENTENCES

EXERCISE

In each of the following examples, combine the sentences into one compound sentence. Make necessary changes.

Example. — It was now the fall of the year, and the nights were cool.

1. It was now the fall of the year. The nights were cool.

2. The leaves turned yellow and brown. The wind caught them up. They danced about.

3. The clouds hung low. They were heavy with hail and snowflakes.

4. One evening, there came a whole flock of great swans out of the bushes. They were shining white. They had long supple necks.

5. The swans uttered a strange cry. They spread forth their great wings. They flew away to warmer lands.

6. The Ugly Duckling had never before seen such beautiful birds. He could not forget them.

LESSON CLXV

LETTER-WRITING

EXERCISE

Write a letter to a boy or a girl in Cuba, and tell —

1. Why the Fourth of July is celebrated in the United States.

2. How it is celebrated.

LESSON CLXVI

DIVIDED QUOTATIONS

EXERCISE 1

Read the following story: —

THE BOY AND THE NETTLES

A boy was stung by a nettle. He ran home and told his mother, saying, "Although it pains me so much, I did but touch it ever so gently."

"That," said his mother, "was just what caused it to sting you. The next time you touch a nettle, grasp it boldly, and it will be as soft as silk to your hand, and will not hurt you in the least."

How many direct quotations[1] do you see in this story? Whose words are repeated in the first quotation? Whose words are repeated in the second?

What words divide the mother's remark into two parts? How are the words, *said his mother*, separated from the remainder of the sentence?

Read the first part of the last quotation. Read the second part. By what is each part enclosed?

When a quotation is divided by other words, each part should be enclosed by quotation marks; as, "The greatest of faults," says Carlyle, "is to be conscious of none."

EXERCISE 2

Copy the story of "The Boy and the Nettles."

[1] See page 56.

LESSON CLXVII

SELECTION TO BE MEMORIZED

THE TREE

The Tree's early leaf-buds were bursting their brown;
" Shall I take them away?" said the Frost, sweeping down.
    " No, leave them alone
    Till the blossoms have grown,"
Prayed the Tree, while he trembled from rootlet to crown.

The Tree bore his blossoms, and all the birds sung;
" Shall I take them away?" said the Wind as he swung.
    " No, leave them alone
    Till the berries have grown,"
Said the Tree, while his leaflets quivering hung.

The Tree bore his fruit in the midsummer glow;
Said the girl, " May I gather thy berries or no?"
    " Yes, all thou canst see, —
    Take them; all are for thee,"
Said the Tree, while he bent down his laden boughs low.
                    — BJÖRNSTJERNE BJÖRNSON.

    What did the frost say to the tree ? What did the tree reply?
    When the tree was in blossom what did the wind ask? What reply did the tree make to the wind?
    When did the girl speak to the tree? What did she ask him? What reply did the tree make ?

EXERCISE

Copy this poem, and commit it to memory.

LESSON CLXVIII

COMPOSITION

EXERCISE 1

Read the following story: —

THE LARK AND HER YOUNG ONES

A lark had built her nest in a wheat-field. The young larks were almost old enough to fly when one day the owner of the field came to see whether the wheat was not ready to cut. He looked over the crop and said, "The wheat is getting ripe, and I must send to all my neighbors to help me with my harvest."

The young larks were very much frightened at this, and asked their mother where they could go for safety. "There is no danger yet," said the mother. "A man who only asks his neighbors to help him in the harvest is not in earnest."

A few days later the owner of the field came again, and found the wheat shedding the grain, as it was over-ripe. This time he said, "I will come to-morrow with all the laborers I can hire, and will harvest this wheat."

When the lark heard this, she said to the young larks, "Now, my children, it is time for us to go. The man is in earnest this time, for he means to cut the wheat himself."

EXERCISE 2

Tell in your own words the story of "The Lark and her Young Ones."

Write in your own words the story of "The Lark and her Young Ones." Be careful to use quotation marks correctly.

LESSON CLXIX

INDIRECT QUOTATIONS

1.   "Bless us," cried the Mayor, "what's that?
    Anything like the sound of a rat
    Makes my heart go pit-a-pat!"

2. The Mayor said that anything like the sound of a rat made his heart go pit-a-pat.

Read the Mayor's words in the first example. Whose remark is repeated in the second example?

When a remark is repeated in the exact words of another, what is the quotation called?

When one person tells what another has said, but does not use the speaker's exact words, the quotation is called an **indirect quotation.**

What kind of quotation do you see in the first example above? What kind in the second example? By what is the direct quotation enclosed?

An indirect quotation should not be enclosed by quotation marks, should not begin with a capital letter, and usually should not be separated from the preceding words by a comma; as, The man said that *he would attend to the matter.*

EXERCISE

Copy the following sentences, and place quotation marks and commas wherever they are needed:—

1. Once more he cried Stop a minute.

2. Charles said that he had received a letter from his uncle.

3. A celebrated writer says Take care of the minutes and the hours will take care of themselves.

4. Herbert says that we planted the seeds too deep.

5. Listen to this boys said she and hear what was done with your letter.

6. This is a pleasant day said Mr. Snow. Does it not make you happy Emily?

7. What did he say to you when he came by asked the officer.

8. He told me that he had to run to save his life.

9.　　　Sisters and brothers, little maid,
　　　　　How many may you be?
　　　How many? Seven in all, she said,
　　　　　And wondering looked at me.

LESSON CLXX
STUDY OF INDIRECT QUOTATIONS
EXERCISE 1

Read the following story:—

MERCURY AND THE WOODMAN

One day while a Woodman was resting from his work by the side of a river, he dropped his axe into the water.

He found it impossible to recover the axe.   Being thus deprived of the means of earning a living, he sat down on the bank and mourned his hard fate.

Mercury, who was passing, asked why he wept.   He told him of the loss of his axe, when Mercury plunged into the water, and bringing up a golden axe, inquired if that were the one he had lost.   Upon the Woodman's saying that it was not his, Mercury disappeared beneath the water a second time, and coming up with a silver axe in his hand, asked the Woodman if that were his.   On the Woodman's saying that this was not his either, Mercury dived into the river for the third time, and brought up the axe that had been lost.   The Woodman said this was his, and he expressed his joy at its recovery.   Mercury was so pleased with the Woodman's honesty that he gave him both the golden and the silver axe in addition to his own.

On his return home the Woodman related to his companions all that had happened.   One of them thought he would see whether he could not secure the same good fortune to himself.   So he ran to the river, threw his axe into the water at the same place, and sat down on the bank to weep.

Mercury appeared as before, and having learned the cause of the Woodman's grief, plunged into the river, brought up a golden axe, and asked him if that were his.   The Woodman seized it greedily and said it was the very same axe that he had lost.   Mercury, displeased at his trickery, not only took away the golden axe, but refused to get for him the axe he had thrown into the water.

EXERCISE 2

(1) *Copy from the foregoing story the sentences which contain indirect quotations.*

(2) *Re-write the sentences copied, using direct quotations in place of the indirect.*

LESSON CLXXI

ORAL COMPOSITION

MERCURY AND THE WOODMAN

EXERCISE

Tell in your own words the story of "Mercury and the Woodman."

LESSON CLXXII

THE COMMA

1. The child has a bright, happy face.
2. Bats have large front teeth.
3. The grocer sells tea, coffee, and sugar.

What does the word *happy* describe? What does *bright* describe? What mark is placed between the two words? What does *front* describe? What kind of *front teeth* do bats have?

The adjectives *bright* and *happy* are used in the same way, — each describes face. The adjectives in the second sentence are not used in the same way; *front* describes *teeth*, but *large* describes *front teeth*.

Words used in the same way are said to be in the **same construction**.

What words in the third sentence are in the same construction? How is each of those words used?

Words or phrases in the same construction should be separated by commas; as, *The lowlands are hot, damp, and unhealthful.*

NOTE. — Two words or two short phrases in the same construction, when connected by a conjunction, should not be separated by a comma; as, *He is tall and slender.*

EXERCISE

Tell which words in the following sentences are in the same construction, and why the commas are used or omitted: —

1. The sky is clear and blue.

2. It will be a clear, cold night.

3. He was in appearance, in manners, and in language a gentleman.

4. We soon forgot the hardships of the long, cold ride.

5. You will find the coat in the hall or in the closet.

6. The cart was filled with potatoes, beets, and cabbages.

7. The surface of the soil is protected by blackbirds, crows, thrushes, and larks.

8. The mountains are covered with forests of pine, fir, and cedar.

LESSON CLXXIII

DICTATION EXERCISE

1. He gave a long, low whistle.

2. The man had a newspaper, a cane, and an umbrella.

3. It was a bright, sunny day.

4. Rover gave a short, quick bark.

5. In the morning we read, sing, and play.

6. Henry, Edwin, and I went to ride.

7. The boy was cold, tired, and hungry.

8. Stone, wood, and brick are used for building houses.

9. Frogs have long hind legs.

10. Chimney swallows build their nests in caves, trees, or chimneys.

11. The streets were crowded with men, women, and children.

12. A small round table stood in the centre of the room.

LESSON CLXXIV
COMPOSITION
USES OF FORESTS

Write about the " Uses of Forests."

1. Tell how forests make, save, and enrich the soil.

2. Show how they prevent floods and droughts.

3. Speak of the value of their timber for manufacturing and heating purposes.

4. Tell how they afford shelter and protection to birds and other animals.

5. Speak of their beauty and grandeur.

LESSON CLXXV
EXPLANATORY EXPRESSIONS

1. Mr. Hall, our new neighbor, was the first one to greet us.

2. Washington, the first President, was buried at Mount Vernon.

Name the subject and the predicate in the first sentence. What is the name of the man spoken of? Who was he?

Who was buried at Mount Vernon? Who was *Washington?*

What is the explanatory part in the first sentence? What in the second sentence? In each sentence what marks separate the explanatory part from the rest of the sentence?

An explanatory expression should be separated from the rest of the sentence by a comma or commas.

EXERCISE

Copy the following sentences, inserting commas where they are needed: —

1. Charles the eldest son has left home.

2. Mr. Curtis the speaker of the evening was delayed by an accident.

3. We heard Mr. Spurgeon the great London preacher.

4. Daniel Webster the great American statesman died at Marshfield.

5. Washington the capital of the United States was named in honor of the first President.

6. San Francisco the largest city in California is noted for its fine harbor.

LESSON CLXXVI

INTERMEDIATE EXPRESSIONS

1. They, *too*, carried a flag.

2. The general, *riding to the front*, led the attack.

3. He has bought, *I hear*, a large tract of land.

Read the first statement. What word is placed between the verb and its subject? How is this word separated from the rest of the sentence?

What is the second statement about? What did the general do? What is the use of the phrase, *riding to the front?* How is it separated from the rest of the sentence?

What is the subject of the verb *has bought?* What is its object? What words are placed between the verb and its object? How are they separated from the rest of the sentence?

Words, phrases, or clauses placed between parts of a sentence closely related, should usually be separated from the rest of the sentence by commas.

EXERCISE

Copy the following sentences, and insert commas where they are needed : —

1. He will no doubt follow your advice.

2. I did him however a great injustice.

3. It is I think the third house from the corner.

4. "My dear Edward" said he "this is truly kind."

5. The book having been read was returned to the library.

6. He was on the whole pleased with the work.

7. The boatman who knew the danger told the passengers to sit still.

8. This was in fact the only interesting feature of the exercises.

9. He has from first to last given us the benefit of his advice.

10. Perhaps too he has forgotten the circumstance.

LESSON CLXXVII

SELECTION TO BE MEMORIZED

Copy the following lines and commit them to memory:—

Thou, too, sail on, O Ship of State!
Sail on, O Union, strong and great!
Humanity with all its fears,
With all the hopes of future years,
Is hanging breathless on thy fate!
We know what master laid thy keel,
What Workmen wrought thy ribs of steel,
Who made each mast, and sail, and rope,
What anvils rang, what hammers beat,
In what a forge and what a heat
Were shaped the anchors of thy hope!
Fear not each sudden sound and shock,
'Tis of the wave and not the rock;
'Tis but the flapping of the sail,
And not a rent made by the gale!
In spite of rock and tempest's roar,
In spite of false lights on the shore,
Sail on, nor fear to breast the sea!
Our hearts, our hopes, are all with thee,
Our hearts, our hopes, our prayers, our tears,
Our faith triumphant o'er our fears,
Are all with thee, — are all with thee!

— HENRY WADSWORTH LONGFELLOW.

LESSON CLXXVIII

LETTER-WRITING

EXERCISE

Write a letter to a boy or a girl who lives in Florida, and tell him or her about the winter sports in your locality.

LESSON CLXXIX

TRANSPOSED EXPRESSIONS

1. The building will be completed in a short time.
2. In a short time, the building will be completed.
3. The flower will fade if you pick it.
4. If you pick the flower, it will fade.

What is said about the building? Mention the verb in this sentence. What phrase modifies the verb *will be completed?* Where is it placed? How does the second sentence differ from the first? How is the phrase separated from the rest of the sentence?

Read the principal clause in the third sentence. Read the dependent clause. Upon what verb does the dependent clause depend? Where is it placed? Where is the dependent clause placed in the fourth sentence? How is it separated from the rest of the sentence?

When a phrase or a clause is placed out of its natural position, it is said to be **transposed.**

A transposed phrase or clause should generally be separated from the rest of the sentence by the comma; as, *Of all our senses, sight is the most perfect and delightful.*

NOTE. — If the phrase is closely united with the sentence, the comma is not used; as, *Beneath the window is a wooden bench.*

EXERCISE

Copy the following sentences, and place commas where they are needed : —

1. Before we could reach the spot the gate was closed.

2. On entering the house he found everything in confusion.

3. In the middle of January he was summoned home.

4. If there were time to spare I should be glad to give you an account of our journey.

5. Without hesitating an instant he stepped forward.

6. If you take my advice you will turn back.

7. When everything was ready the doors were thrown open.

8. One cold winter night a knock came at the door.

9. As he entered the city he noticed the many changes that had taken place since his last visit.

10. In skating over thin ice safety lies in speed.

11. If he would listen to the explanation he would understand the matter.

12. In the first place it must be shown that this building is needed.

13. When the news was received there was great rejoicing among the people.

14. If all goes well the work will soon be completed.

LESSON CLXXX

STUDY OF SELECTION

THE DAFFODILS

I

I wandered lonely as a cloud
  That floats on high o'er vales and hills,
When all at once I saw a crowd,
  A host, of golden daffodils;
    Beside the lake, beneath the trees,
    Fluttering and dancing in the breeze.

II

Continuous as the stars that shine
  And twinkle on the Milky Way,
They stretched in never-ending line
  Along the margin of a bay:
    Ten thousand saw I at a glance,
    Tossing their heads in sprightly dance.

III

The waves beside them danced; but they
  Outdid the sparkling waves in glee:
A poet could not but be gay,
  In such a jocund company:
    I gazed, — and gazed, — but little thought
    What wealth the show to me had brought:

IV

For oft, when on my couch I lie
In vacant or in pensive mood,
They flash upon that inward eye
Which is the bliss of solitude;
And then my heart with pleasure fills,
And dances with the daffodils.

— WILLIAM WORDSWORTH.

Read the first stanza. Who is meant by *I*? Why is *wandered* used instead of *walked*? What is the use of *lonely*? To what is the loneliness of the poet compared? What is the office of the second line? To what does *that* refer? What do the next two lines tell? Where were the daffodils? What is the office of the · last line?

Read the second stanza. What do the first four lines describe? How were the daffodils arranged? What is the meaning of *margin*? Does the poet mean that he saw exactly ten thousand? What does he mean? What are the daffodils said to be doing?

Read the third stanza. What waves are spoken of? What did the waves do? In what did the daffodils surpass the waves? What is the meaning of the third and fourth lines? What do the last two lines tell?

Read the last stanza. Read the principal clause in the first statement. When do *they flash upon the inward eye*? What is a *vacant* mood? What is the meaning of *pensive*? What does the fourth line describe? Give in your own words the meaning of the first four lines of this stanza. What feeling did this sight awaken in the mind of the poet?

EXERCISE 1

Make a list of all the words in this poem that express motion, and notice how their use adds to the vividness of the description.

EXERCISE 2

Write sentences illustrating the correct use of the following words : —

wandered	lonely	floats	host
golden	beside	beneath	fluttering
dancing	continuous	margin	bay
glance	sprightly	glee	jocund
mood	vacant	pensive	solitude

EXERCISE 3

Copy the poem, and commit it to memory.

LESSON CLXXXI

REVIEW OF PUNCTUATION

DICTATION EXERCISE

I, poor, miserable Robinson Crusoe, being shipwrecked, came on shore on this dismal, unfortunate island.

I had neither food, house, clothes, weapon, nor place to fly to; and feared that I should be devoured by wild beasts, murdered by savages, or starved to death for want of food. At the approach of night, I slept in a tree, for fear of wild creatures; but slept soundly, though it rained all night.

In the morning I saw, to my great surprise, that the ship had floated with the high tide, and was driven on shore again much nearer to the island. I hoped, if the wind abated, I might get on board, and get some food and necessaries out of her for my relief. At length, seeing the ship almost dry, I went upon the sand as near as I could, and then swam on board.

— ADAPTED FROM " ROBINSON CRUSOE."

LESSON CLXXXII

COMPOSITION

THANKSGIVING DAY

Write an account of Thanksgiving Day, using the following outline : —

1. The origin of Thanksgiving Day.

2. How the day was observed by the early New England settlers.

3. Who appoints our Thanksgiving Day, and how the day is observed.

4. The benefits derived from its observance.

LESSON CLXXXIII

A BUSINESS LETTER

Study the following letter carefully, noting the arrangement of its different parts (see page 38) — the **heading,** the **address,** the **salutation,** the **body of the letter,** and the conclusion : —

95 STATE STREET, CLEVELAND, OHIO,
December 12, 1908.

THE CENTURY CO.,
· UNION SQUARE,
NEW YORK.

DEAR SIRS:

Enclosed is a money order for three dollars, for which please send me "St. Nicholas" for one year, beginning with the next number.

Yours truly,

CHARLES R. HOWARD.

Observe that this letter is more formal than the one given on page 37. The address of the firm written to is placed at the beginning of the letter, on the first line below the heading, and a formal salutation is used.

Notice also that this letter contains no matter not relating to the sending of the subscription. A business letter should give in a clear and concise manner whatever pertains to the special subject of the letter, but nothing more.

EXERCISE 1

Copy the foregoing letter carefully, paying particular attention to capital letters, marks of punctuation, and the arrangement of the different parts of the letter.

EXERCISE 2

Write to The Century Co., Union Square, N.Y., subscribing for " St. Nicholas," which is to be sent to one of your friends. Use real names and addresses in your letter.

EXERCISE 3

Write to the publisher of your local newspaper, notifying him that the daily paper has not been left at your door for the last two days.

EXERCISE 4

You are planning a flower garden. Write to Wild, Rose & Co., Geneva, N.Y., and ask them to send you a catalogue, describing the seeds and plants which they have for sale.

EXERCISE 5

You desire to enter a public school in a neighboring town. Write to the principal of the school, asking him upon what terms non-resident pupils may be admitted to the school.

LESSON CLXXXIV

REPORTS OF BIRD STUDIES

Study a bird that may be found in the streets or the fields near your home, and then write out a report of your observations.

Tell the size of the bird, its colors, and the place where it is most frequently seen. State in particular anything that you have learned of its habits, and describe its song.

If you have discovered the bird's nest, tell where it was placed, how it was constructed, and how many eggs it contained. State the color of the eggs.

Among birds that may be easily observed are the following : —

Robin	Baltimore Oriole
Bluebird	Meadow-lark
Catbird	Woodpecker

LESSON CLXXXV

REPORTS OF TREE STUDIES

Describe a tree of one of the varieties named in the following list, or a tree of any other kind that grows near your home.

State its comparative height, and the general appearance of its trunk and its branches. Describe in particular the color and the surface of its bark.

Describe the size, the form, and the color of its leaves, and tell how they are arranged on the stem.

Tell when its flowers appear, whether before or after the leaves, and describe the flowers.

Describe the fruit (the part of the tree that contains the seed), tell when it ripens, and whether it falls to the ground early in the season or remains on the tree through the winter.

Among interesting trees for study are the following : —

American Elm	Oak
Hickory	Pine
Locust	Poplar
Maple	Willow

LESSON CLXXXVI

STORIES FROM OUTLINES

Write a short story suggested by one of the following topics. Follow the outline given.

EXERCISE 1

A STRAY CHILD

1. When and where the child was first seen, and by whom
2. Her appearance, and what she said about herself.
3. What was done with her.

EXERCISE 2

A PARROT ON A STREET CAR

1. Who brought the parrot into the car.
2. What the parrot did and said.
3. What the effect was on the passengers.

EXERCISE 3

AN AFTERNOON TRAMP

1. Who went.
2. Where they went.
3. What they saw and did.

EXERCISE 4

HELEN'S BIRTHDAY PARTY

1. Who Helen was and where she lived.
2. Who were invited to her party.

3. How the children were entertained.
4. Where and how the supper was served.
5. The best thing about her party.

EXERCISE 5

ROBERT'S LETTER TO SANTA CLAUS

1. Who Robert was.
2. How he came to write to Santa Claus.
3. How his letter was answered.

LESSON CLXXXVII

DESCRIPTIONS FROM OUTLINES

Write a description of some interesting place or scene suggested by one of the following topics. Give such details as will help the reader to see what you saw.

EXERCISE 1

A CITY STREET

1. Where it was.
2. What made it interesting.

EXERCISE 2

AN OLD-FASHIONED GARDEN

1. How it was laid out — in beds, walks, etc.
2. What kinds of flowers it contained.
3. How the different plants were arranged.
4. The most attractive spot in the garden.

EXERCISE 3

A SUMMER CAMP

1. Its location and surroundings.
2. The tents and their furnishings.
3. The members of the camping party.
4. How the members spend their time.

EXERCISE 4

A COUNTRY FAIR

1. The grounds.
2. The different classes of articles on exhibition — live-stock, machinery, fruit, flowers, vegetables, and other articles.
3. Special features of interest.

EXERCISE 5

A CITY POST-OFFICE

1. Its different departments.
2. Its collection of mail matter.
3. Its delivery of mail matter.

LESSON CLXXXVIII

STUDY OF A POEM

THE SONG OF THE BROOK

(From "The Brook")

I come from haunts of coot and hern,
I make a sudden sally,
And sparkle out among the fern,
To bicker down a valley.

By thirty hills I hurry down,
  Or slip between the ridges,
By twenty thorps, a little town,
  And half a hundred bridges.

Till last by Philip's farm I flow
  To join the brimming river,
For men may come and men may go,
  But I go on forever.

I chatter over stony ways,
  In little sharps and trebles,
I bubble into eddying bays,
  I babble on the pebbles.

With many a curve my banks I fret
  By many a field and fallow,
And many a fairy foreland set
  With willow-weed and mallow.

I chatter, chatter, as I flow
  To join the brimming river,
For men may come and men may go,
  But I go on forever.

I wind about, and in and out,
  With here a blossom sailing,
And here and there a lusty trout,
  And here and there a grayling,

And here and there a foamy flake
  Upon me as I travel
With many a silvery waterbreak
  Above the golden gravel,

And draw them all along, and flow
  To join the brimming river,
For men may come and men may go,
  But I go on forever.

I steal by lawns and grassy plots,
  I slide by hazel covers;
I move the sweet forget-me-nots
  That grow for happy lovers.

I slip, I slide, I gloom, I glance,
  Among the skimming swallows;
I make the netted sunbeam dance
  Against my sandy shallows.

I murmur under moon and stars
  In brambly wildernesses;
I linger by my shingly bars;
  I loiter round my cresses;

And out again I curve and flow
  To join the brimming river,
For men may come and men may go,
  But I go on forever.

                    —ALFRED TENNYSON.

Read this poem carefully, and try to imagine the course of the brook. Where did the brook come from? What is a *coot?* A *hern?* What is the meaning of *haunts?*

Mention the different things that the brook passed on its way to the river.

Point out the different words in this poem that show the movement of the brook. What words suggest the sound made by the water? What words or phrases bring pleasant pictures before your mind?

EXERCISE

Copy the poem, and commit it to memory.

LESSON CLXXXIX

SELECTIONS TO BE MEMORIZED

Copy the following selections, and commit to memory the lines that you like the best: —

I

The year's at the spring
And day's at the morn;
Morning's at seven;
The hillside's dew-pearled;
The lark's on the wing;
The snail's on the thorn:
God's in his heaven —
All's right with the world!

— ROBERT BROWNING.

II

'Tis enough for us now that the leaves are green;
We sit in the warm shade and feel right well
How the sap creeps up and the blossoms swell;
We may shut our eyes, but we cannot help knowing
That skies are clear and grass is growing;
The breeze comes whispering in our ear,
That dandelions are blossoming near,

That maize has sprouted, that streams are flowing,
That the river is bluer than the sky,
That the robin is plastering his house hard by;
And if the breeze kept the good news back,
For other couriers we should not lack;

We could guess it all by yon heifer's lowing, —
And hark! how clear bold chanticleer,
Warmed with the new wine of the year,
Tells all in his lusty crowing!

—JAMES RUSSELL LOWELL.

III

When icicles hang by the wall,
And Dick the shepherd blows his nail,
And Tom bears logs into the hall,
And milk comes frozen home in pail,
When blood is nipp'd and ways be foul,
Then nightly sings the staring owl,
Tu-whit;
Tu-who, a merry note,
While greasy Joan doth keel the pot.

—WILLIAM SHAKESPEARE.

LIST OF ABBREVIATIONS

Ala. . . . . Alabama.	**Ind.** . . . . Indiana.
A.M. Before noon (*ante meridiem*).	**Ind. T.** . . . . Indian Territory.
Ark. . . . . Arkansas.	**Iowa** or **Io.** . . . . . . Iowa.
Ariz. . . . . Arizona.	**Jan** . . . . January.
Aug. . . . . August.	**Jr.** or **Jun.** . . . . Junior.
Av. or **Ave.** . . . . . Avenue.	**Kans.** or **Kan.** . . . . Kansas.
Cal. . . . . California.	**Ky.** . . . . Kentucky.
Capt. . . . . Captain.	**La.** . . . . Louisiana.
Co. . . . . Company.	**L.I.** . . . . . . Long Island.
Co. . . . . County.	**Lieut.** . . . . . . Lieutenant.
Col. . . . . Colonel.	**LL.D.** . . . . Doctor of Laws.
Colo. or **Col.** . . . . . Colorado.	**M.** . . . . . . Noon (*meridies*).
Conn. . . . . . . Connecticut.	**Mass.** . . . . . Massachusetts.
D.C. . . . . District of Columbia.	**M.C.** . . . . Member of Congress.
D.D. . . . . Doctor of Divinity.	**M.D.** . . . . Doctor of Medicine.
Dec. . . . . December.	**Md.** . . . . Maryland.
Del. . . . . Delaware.	**Me.** . . . . Maine.
Dr. . . . . Doctor.	**Messrs.** . . Gentlemen (*Messieurs*).
E. . . . . East.	**Mich.** . . . . . . Michigan.
Esq. . . . . Esquire.	**Minn.** . . . . . . Minnesota.
Feb. . . . . February.	**Miss.** . . . . . . Mississippi.
Fla. . . . . Florida.	**Mo.** . . . . Missouri.
Fri. . . . . Friday.	**Mon.** . . . . . . Monday.
Ga. . . . . Georgia.	**Mont.** . . . . . . Montana.
Gen. . . . . General.	**Mr.** . . . . Mister.
Gov. . . . . Governor.	**Mrs.** . . . . Mistress.
Hon. . . . . . . Honorable.	**Mt.** . . . . Mount.
Idaho . . . . Idaho.	**N.** . . . . North.
Ill. . . . . Illinois.	**N.A.** . . . . . North America.

Nebr. or **Neb.** . . . . . Nebraska.	**R.R.** . . . . Railroad.
Nev. . . . . Nevada.	**S.** . . . . South.
N.C. . . . . . North Carolina.	**Sat.** . . . . Saturday.
N. Dak. . . . . . . North Dakota.	**Sept.** . . . . September.
N.H. . . . . . New Hampshire.	**Sr.** or **Sen.** . . . . . Senior.
N.J. . . . . New Jersey.	**S.C.** . . . . . . South Carolina.
N. Mex. . . . . . New Mexico.	**S. Dak.** . . . . . South Dakota.
No. . . . . Number.	**St.** . . . . Street.
Nov. . . . . November.	**Sun.** . . . . Sunday.
N.Y. . . . . New York.	**Supt.** . . . . . Superintendent.
Ohio or **O.** . . . . Ohio.	**Tenn.** . . . . Tennessee.
Oct. . . . . October.	**Tex.** . . . . Texas.
Okla. . . . . Oklahoma.	**Thurs.** . . . . Thursday.
Or. . . . . Oregon.	**Tues.** . . . . Tuesday.
p. . . . . Page.	**U.S.** . . . . United States.
Pa. or **Penn.** . . . . Pennsylvania.	**Utah** . . . . Utah.
Ph. D. . . . Doctor of Philosophy.	**Va.** . . . . Virginia.
P.M. . Afternoon (*post meridiem*).	**Vt.** . . . . Vermont.
P.M. . . . . Postmaster.	**W.** . . . . West.
P.O. . . . . Post-Office.	**Wash.** . . . . . . Washington.
Pres. . . . . President.	**Wed.** . . . . . . Wednesday.
Prof. . . . . Professor.	**Wis.** . . . . Wisconsin.
P.S. . . . Postscript (*post scriptum*).	**Wyo.** . . . . Wyoming.
Rev. . . . . Reverend.	**W. Va.** . . . . West Virginia.
R.I. . . . . Rhode Island.	

INDEX